Representing
Yourself

Also by Kenneth Lasson

*The Workers: Portraits of
Nine American Jobholders*

*Proudly We Hail: Profiles of
Public Citizens in Action*

Private Lives of Public Servants

Your Rights and the Draft

Your Rights as a Vet

Getting the Most Out of Washington
(with Senator William Cohen)

Also from Public Citizen

*Pills That Don't Work: A Consumers' and
Doctors' Guide to Prescription Drugs That
Lack Evidence of Effectiveness*

*The X-ray Information Book: A Consumers'
Guide to Avoiding Unnecessary Medical
and Dental X-rays* (with Priscilla W. Laws,
Ph.D.)

REPRESENTING YOURSELF

What You Can Do Without a Lawyer

Kenneth Lasson
and the
Public Citizen Litigation Group

Introduction by Ralph Nader

Farrar · Straus · Giroux / *New York*

Copyright © 1983 by Kenneth Lasson and
the Public Citizen Litigation Group

ALL RIGHTS RESERVED

Second printing, 1983

PRINTED IN THE UNITED STATES OF AMERICA

Published simultaneously in Canada by
McGraw-Hill Ryerson Ltd., Toronto

DESIGNED BY STEPHEN DYER

Library of Congress Cataloging in Publication Data

Lasson, Kenneth.
Representing yourself.
Bibliography: p.
1. Pro se representation—United States—Popular
works. I. Public Citizen Litigation Group. II. Title.
KF8841.L27   1983   346'.73'013   83–1406
ISBN 0–374–24943–1   347.30613
ISBN 0–374–51726–6 (pbk.)

For Barbara

WE are grateful to a number of people for their assistance in preparation of the manuscript. Principal among them are Katharine Thurlow and Marc Nachman, Esquires (research); Nancy Miller (editorial comments); Arthur Fox, Mark Sargent, Charles Shafer, John Sims, William Weston, and Sidney Wolfe (notes on the manuscript); and Ella Agambar (typing). We are particularly indebted to Alan B. Morrison of Public Citizen for his thorough reading of and extensive comments on various drafts of the manuscript.

Contents

Using the Federal Government

Hiring a Lawyer

Introduction

by Ralph Nader

> *Discourage litigation. Persuade your neighbors*
> *to compromise whenever you can . . . As a*
> *peace-maker the lawyer has a superior op-*
> *portunity of being a good man. There will still*
> *be business enough.*
>
> —Abraham Lincoln
> NOTES FOR LAW LECTURE

THERE are enough criticisms against lawyers without this book needing to contribute to the broadside—but let it be understood that much of what has been written publicly and grumbled privately is fully warranted. The image of the legal profession—which should reflect an overriding concern for fairness, justice, and equality—has instead been tarnished by greed, complacency, and self-righteousness. That America is the most litigious country on earth is due at least in part to our excess of lawyers, nurturing the presumption that grievances can best be redressed by going to court. The United States produces some 40,000 new attorneys a year and accounts for two thirds of all the lawyers in the world (three times as many per capita as England, twenty-one times as many as Japan). To put it simply, they need the work. The unfortunate result of such pragmatism is that lawyers often get in the way of amicable resolutions of disputes, and they serve as needless middlemen in a wide variety of common legal problems—from the probate of wills (for which the British seldom use lawyers) to the settlement of real-estate transactions (which usually require little more expertise than simple common sense).

Lawyers like to say the law is a jealous mistress—maybe that's why lawyers are so expensive, and consequently tend to be most utilized by the well-heeled. The rich are perceived as getting richer through the foxy devices of tax attorneys paid hefty fees to find loopholes (or lobby for their enactment). Law students are trained much more heavily in the technicalities of corporations, securities, creditors' rights, and commercial transactions than they are in consumerism, tenants' and debtors' rights, or the ethics of dispute prevention or resolution. Despite the overabundance of lawyers, it's still hard to find one who will handle a low-paying case. In fact, until minimum-fee schedules and rules against competitive advertising were recently ruled illegal, the consumer was even more a victim of the legal establishment's self-regulated monopoly.

None of this, however, should demean the hardworking attorneys who serve useful, important, and often absolutely necessary purposes. Nor should it suggest that being a lawyer makes one any *less* ethical than being a doctor, plumber, or bureaucrat. (Whether we in the profession like to admit it or not, compassion and integrity are reflections of one's character and upbringing much more than of one's education.)

But there are some very good reasons to pause before running to the nearest lawyer at the first mention of contract or blush of confrontation. Many businessmen insist they operate more effectively on handshake agreements than written legal documents. Even where a written contract is necessary, or simply judicious, it can frequently be drafted by Party A and Party B themselves. Relatively minor arguments over rights, duties, and damages might better be settled after passions have cooled than through a heated "My lawyer will contact you in the morning!" In a great many cases, all that's needed is a cool-headed third party (a role which can also be played by an attorney). Indeed, a trend is developing toward the use of divorce counselors or mediators rather than lawyers in cases where both spouses seek a peaceful dissolution of their marriage.

In short, with lawyers' hourly fees soaring into the triple digits and their professional image continuing to plummet, more and more Americans wonder if there might be an alternative to seeking an attorney when they face legal problems. The answer is often yes.

At the Public Citizen Litigation Group, a public-interest law firm we founded in 1972, letters arrive nearly every day from consumers unhappy with negligent, condescending, dishonest, or, most often, expensive attorneys. On several occasions Public Citizen has itself brought suit to establish principles that would make legal services available to more people at affordable prices. One of the first cases initiated by the Litigation Group was *Goldfarb v. Virginia State Bar*, in which the Supreme Court of the United States found that the bar's rule *requiring* its attorneys to charge a minimum fee for routine legal services violated the federal antitrust laws. Public Citizen also participated in the suit in which the Supreme Court held that lawyers have a First Amendment right to advertise. Both decisions have served to increase competition among attorneys, encourage the development of legal clinics, and thereby reduce fees.

Public Citizen likewise challenged the restrictions on nonlawyers who wish to help others pursue their rights. In Florida, the group represented a legal secretary who for several years had been helping husbands and wives prepare the forms necessary to obtain a divorce. In Virginia, it sued the bar on behalf of a title-insurance company which had offered low-cost house settlements to home buyers by hiring nonlawyers to do most of the simple work involved. In Wisconsin, one of Public Citizen's clients is an environmental activist who represents his group before state agencies, over the bar's objection that he never went to law school.

In fact, many tasks that lawyers perform are routine, and reasonably intelligent citizens who have the time should be able to do things like conduct their own house settlement, file for a simple divorce, or draft a simple will. The principal goal of this book is to demystify the law, and to suggest the many ways by which people can be their own best lawyers.

To be sure, many problems require a good lawyer's assistance—no one with a large estate, for example, should write a will without benefit of counsel, nor should you defend yourself against a criminal charge. But a careful perusal of the pages that follow should help readers ask the right questions, get the best service, and—perhaps most important—decide whether they really need a lawyer at all.

Your Property

1

Contracts

Make every bargain clear and plain,
That none may afterwards complain.
                    —John Ray, ENGLISH PROVERBS

CONTRACTS are the most common, yet most commonly misunderstood, of legal transactions. When people think of contracts, they envision thick sheaves of heavy paper filled with fine print and jargon: parties of the first part, wherefores, and whatnots. Few realize that most of us make contracts every day of our lives, without the need for such incomprehensible words—or any written instruments at all.

Consider the following scenario:

Phoebe reaches Virginia on the telephone late Monday evening. "Can you babysit for Willy on Saturday night? Edgar and I want to see a movie."

"Sure," says Virginia. "What time?"

"Why don't we say 7:30. We'll pick you up."

"Okay. See you then."

Phoebe and Virginia have just made a contract—just as millions of others do every day without knowing it. The terms of their babysitting agreement were not spelled out in a formal document, but they are reasonably clear to the parties who made them. (Lawyers often use words in contracts and other

3

documents that many people don't understand—hence, the glossary at the end of this book.) Virginia has agreed to sit for Phoebe and Edgar on Saturday night, forgoing other opportunities, like visiting with friends or babysitting for someone else who might pay a little more money. Phoebe and Edgar, on the other hand, have obligated themselves to pay Virginia for her time, perhaps even if they decide to cancel at the last minute.

Most of the terms of this agreement are unstated. The only item that was actually mentioned—the *express* term—was the time Phoebe would pick up Virginia at her home. Everything else in the agreement is *implied*.

For instance, no mention was made of a specific hourly rate. Yet both sides obviously had expectations as to what the figures would be, probably because Virginia used to sit regularly for Phoebe and Edgar or because there is a "going rate" which all babysitters receive in the neighborhood.

There are other implied terms. Unless Virginia lives within walking distance, Phoebe and Edgar are obligated to pick her up and drive her home. For her part, Virginia must do more than just "sit"; she has to take care of the needs of the child, see that he brushes his teeth, and probably read him a story before tucking him in at bedtime. On the other hand, she also has certain unstated rights—to watch television when Willy is in bed, to do her homework or read a book, to have a glass of milk (but probably not a beer), and to sample the contents of the cookie jar. All those implied terms are very much part of the contract, because they are part of the understanding that all people who enter into these kinds of agreements—babysitters and parents alike—accept as the operative rules.

The essence of a contract is an exchange of promises. Contracts must be mutual. Thus, if someone offers to cut your lawn for $10, you are not obligated to pay unless you accept the offer. A promise can also take the form of giving up something, such as not using your power lawn mower on Saturday morning, in exchange for the right to use your neighbor's pool on Sunday afternoon.

Regardless of the form of the contract, for it to be valid, both sides must part with something of value. This is called *consideration*. Thus, if a janitor, who is paid by the landlord to pick up trash, tells a particular tenant that he will empty his wastebaskets only if the tenant pays him an extra $5 a week, the tenant's promise to pay would be unenforceable because the janitor is already obligated to do the job without the additional payment.

The amount of consideration is generally irrelevant. If Sam offers to sell his 1954 Studebaker to Joe for $10,000, and if Joe agrees, but then changes his mind because he thinks the price is too high, the courts will probably not get involved in the controversy, unless there is fraud or some special circumstance. In legal terms, the courts say that they will not examine the *adequacy of consideration*—which means they won't try to second-guess the parties about whether one gave up too much or received too little. In other words, if you make a bad bargain, you are stuck with the results. (There are some exceptions, most notably minimum-wage laws, which are designed to protect those who are in a bad bargaining position and may need a job so badly that they would be willing to work for less than what the law says is a fair wage.)

Some contracts have to be in writing to be enforceable. The vast majority of contracts are not written but are simply agreed upon by an exchange of spoken words or a shake of the hand. Make no mistake about them—such verbal agreements are enforceable. Thus, if you go to the best restaurant in the city and order the highest-priced meal and the most expensive wine, you are legally obligated to pay for the meal even though nothing was written down or signed by you.

However, there are a few contracts which can be enforced *only* if they are in writing and if you have signed a piece of paper accepting their terms. The most important of these are contracts for the purchase of land (or a long-term lease), an agreement to pay someone else's debts, or a purchase of goods over a certain amount (generally $500 to $1,000, depending on your state's law). In addition, contracts that require one side to perform a service or supply goods over a long period of time (such as a year) also generally have to be in writing before you can seek damages in court.

There are several reasons why the law requires these agreements to be written. Generally, they involve important matters, such as the purchase of real estate, or they relate to matters over which confusion could often arise, such as whether your rich uncle really did mean to promise to pay your debts if you don't.

But there is another reason why important contracts generally should be in writing: it greatly reduces disputes over who promised what to whom. It is a well-known fact that people usually remember what's most favorable to them and that disputes often arise because people hear things they want to hear and forget those that seem unsuited to their circumstances. Putting the terms of an agreement in writing also helps ensure that the parties focus on all the terms of the agreement and thus considerably narrows the potential for controversy. There may still be disputes, since few of us ever express ourselves as clearly as we would like, and no one can think of every contingency. But putting it in writing helps.

Like almost everything else in contracts, it's generally up to you to decide whether to insist that the agreement be reduced to writing. The best advice is to use common sense: if it's important, if there are a lot of special conditions, or if you've never dealt with the other person before, it's probably worth the time, trouble, and expense to put it down on paper. On the other hand, in an everyday situation like a babysitting arrangement, demand for a written agreement would be out of place.

Note that it is never *illegal* to make a verbal contract for the sale of land to another or to agree by handshake to shovel a neighbor's walk whenever it snows during the next three years, for $10. In fact, many such agreements are made and fully carried out every day. But if there is a dispute about the agreement, a court won't enforce the promise made by the other side unless it is in writing.

The terms of the contract are up to you. In general, the parties can decide on the terms of their contracts themselves. With very few exceptions, the parties, not the law, dictate what will be in the contract. Virginia was free to tell Phoebe that she would not sit for less than $5 an hour, and Phoebe could have said that she would pay no more than $1 an hour (since the minimum-wage laws don't apply to that kind of babysitting arrangement). If the parties agreed on either rate, that was fine, and, most important, if they didn't agree, then there was no contract. In other words, it's entirely up to you whether you want to enter into a contract, and if so, on what terms.

Another example: The store where you bought this book was free to offer to sell it to you at the cover price, at less than the cover price, or at more than the cover price; you were free to accept that offer or not buy the book. If the store refused to accept your check or credit card but insisted on cash, it was up to you to decide whether that term in the contract was satisfactory to you. In short, there are virtually no contract terms forbidden by law, provided that both sides agree to them.

There are a few exceptions to this general rule. The law, however, will not enforce illegal contracts, such as a promise to pay $10,000 to a "hit man" to murder your spouse. Similarly, and more commonly, the courts will not help a winner in a card game collect the money the loser borrowed, lost, and now won't pay back. The law also recognizes that in some circumstances the bargaining positions of the parties may be so unequal, and the price exacted so high, as to be unconscionable;

such promises will likewise not be enforced. (See Chapter 4 on defective products.)

The promises of certain categories of people are not enforceable against them. In order to enter a binding contract, you must have what is known as the *legal capacity* to do so. Certain groups of people, principally those who are judged not to have sufficiently sound judgment to decide important things for themselves, can sign contracts as they please, but the courts won't hold them to their promises.

The largest group of persons who in general are considered not to have the capacity to enter into binding agreements are minors—people under the legal age, which is usually between eighteen and twenty-one, but varies from state to state. Agreements made by minors are not enforceable *against* them. That's why parents of minors are generally asked to co-sign a contract when, for instance, a teenager wants to buy a car. In that case, even though the minor cannot be made to pay, the parents can. Since laws relating to legal capacity are intended to protect minors and others such as the mentally unsound or the intoxicated, promises made by other parties to a transaction are generally enforceable against them but not enforceable against the legally incapacitated.

On this issue, however, the law is not entirely a one-way street. Thus, a sixteen-year-old who goes to a restaurant and eats a meal and refuses to pay on the grounds that he is a minor can't get away with it. This is a notable exception whereby a minor's contracting for necessities such as food and basic clothing is enforceable against him. Indeed, in some cases, not only is the minor required to pay, but so are his parents.

Beware of contract modifications. A contract modification is a change in terms after both parties have agreed and, in the case of a written contract, signed. Sometimes modifications are no more than clarifications of ambiguities that the parties first recognize after the contract is signed. In other instances, the change may be more basic, such as an increase in price on the work the carpenter promised to do in repairing your screen porch.

In some states, an agreement to modify a prior contract must be supported by an additional promise on both sides or it is not enforceable. Thus, if I have promised to mow your lawn for $5 every week during the summer, your promise to pay me $6 is not enforceable unless I have promised to do something extra for you. Of course, there is nothing to prevent you from paying me the extra dollar a week, but in some states you can hold me to my original price. In most instances, however, contracts require the mutual cooperation of both parties, and thus it makes sense to make changes when fairness dictates.

You don't need a lawyer to enter into a contract. If you did, life would grind toward a halt, and we would spend all our time consulting with lawyers every time we bought a newspaper, ordered a meal, or got on a bus.

Nonetheless, it is far preferable to have lawyers prepare certain kinds of contracts—especially when the agreement is complicated, or when there is a great deal of money at stake.

Lawyers have two important skills that are helpful in making contracts. First, they are trained to write clearly and precisely and to remove ambiguities that can lead to later disputes. Second, they are used to anticipating problems and making certain that all the essential elements of the agreement are spelled out.

For instance, you could enter into a written contract under which someone would paint your barn by the end of the next month for $500. That sounds like a perfectly straightforward contract, but a good lawyer would ask, "Who's going to pay for the paint?" If the paint were to run $100 or so, the answer to that question would likely make a difference to both parties. The answer may be clear, if the other party is in the painting business, because in most places the custom is for the painter to supply the paint. But if the painter is a college student home on vacation, it's much less likely that he would expect to supply the paint. In this case, anticipating the problem may mean that there will be no agreement, because each side wants the other to pay for the paint. But surely it is far better for that difference to be known before the work is done, rather than after.

There are a few essential elements to bear in mind if you are writing your own contract. First and most important, keep it simple. Avoid legalese. If you don't know what a word means, don't put it in just because you saw it in some form contract that you bought at the stationery store. Try to provide for all expected contingencies, but remember that even the best lawyers can't think of everything all of the time.

Be sure to put the date on the contract, particularly if there is more than one version or if there are modifications. If a dispute occurs later on, the dates may help explain what otherwise would be contradictions, and may make clear what the final agreement was between the parties.

There is no one magic form for a contract. Anything which demonstrates that the parties have reached an agreement and which sets forth the essential terms will do. One of the simplest forms of a contract is a letter from one party to the other stating his understanding of the agreement. If you choose this method, enclose an extra copy of the letter, and ask the other party to sign and return it if the terms are acceptable.

When in doubt, have your lawyer look it over. Lawyers can and often do prepare contracts for others. But since most lawyers charge more if they do more work, and since drafting a contract can be time-consuming, you may have to pay a lawyer a considerable amount of money if he or she actually prepares the document.

Lawyers can perform a very useful function—at a greatly reduced cost—if you simply ask them to look at your contract after you and the other side have agreed, but before you sign on the dotted line. This is especially important if the other side has a lawyer or if the contract is on a printed form prepared by a bank or insurance company. Good lawyers can read an agreement and let you know if they see any problems. And they can do it in far less time than it would have taken if they did all the work from scratch. Thus, for a relatively small price, you can have peace of mind, knowing that you have signed a reasonable contract or that you ought to consider changing it to add some protections or make some clarifications. Again, if the contract is moderately complicated or considerable money is involved, a relatively small payment to a lawyer can be the best investment you can make.

2

Landlord-Tenant Relations

A good lawyer, a bad neighbor.
—Benjamin Franklin
POOR RICHARD'S ALMANACK

DISPUTES between landlords and tenants are so common that many jurisdictions have special courts to resolve them. But leases are basically like other contracts. In fact, except for a few special rules not applicable to other contracts, a lease is no different from the babysitting contract between Phoebe and Virginia. Each term must be agreed to by both parties, all of them are subject to change, and unless there is a mutual agreement, then neither the landlord nor the tenant has to sign. The fact that a typical apartment lease is on a printed form, requiring a magnifying glass to read it, doesn't alter this principle.

Two things make leases a little different. First, they often include unfamiliar terms which have acquired significant meanings that, unless changed, may drastically affect your rights. Second, custom plays a major role in interpreting leases. Thus, in the absence of specific provisions to the contrary, the law often implies terms in a lease that do not appear anywhere in writing. Not too surprisingly, these two factors generally (but not always) favor landlords.

There are three basic kinds of landlord-tenant arrangements (called "tenancies"): a tenancy for years, a tenancy for a fixed period, and a tenancy at will or at sufferance.

A *tenancy for years* is created by a long-term written lease that is set to expire at a specific date. The term of the lease is generally a year or longer, and when the term ends, the lease expires automatically, without the need for either party to give notice.

A *tenancy for a fixed period* (often called a *periodic tenancy*) is created when a lease runs from one period of time to the next like period (typically, month to month), until it is terminated by one party's notice to the other that the tenancy will not be renewed. The period when it is a month or a week, rather than a year, is generally the interval in which the rent is paid. The beginning date of such an arrangement must be specific, but the termination date is left open until the time that proper notice is given. The meaning of the term *proper notice* should be described in the lease, but it generally ranges from one week to two months, depending on the length of the period of the lease.

A *tenancy at will or at sufferance* is an informal arrangement in which either party can terminate the tenancy without breaking their promises. Generally, there is no written lease. At common law, neither the landlord nor the tenant had to give any prior notice of an intention to end the arrangement. The landlord could send the tenant a notice to leave the premises immediately; the tenant could likewise abandon whenever he wanted to. Today most states have passed laws which require the landlord to give some sort of notice prior to terminating a tenancy at will. State laws vary, however, and required notice could be anything from a week's to a month's notice, often depending upon the way the rental payments are made. (The required notice seldom exceeds thirty days.)

Your rights may depend on the type of tenancy you have. The type of lease primarily affects (a) the ease with which either party can terminate it without being liable for damages for breach of contract, and (b) the manner in which a landlord can raise the rental payments. Unless otherwise provided in the lease, the amount of rent is assumed to remain unchanged during the period of the lease in a tenancy for years. In contrast, in a tenancy at will or a periodic tenancy, the landlord is generally free to increase the rent simply by giving the same notice as would be required to terminate the tenancy.

The type of tenancy also determines what effect, if any, the sale of the property to a new owner has upon the tenant. In either a tenancy for years or a periodic tenancy, the new owner has no right to evict any tenant (except for a breach of the lease) until the period of the lease expires or proper notice is given. Nor can a new owner singlehandedly change the terms of an existing lease. The tenant has the right (and the duty) to perform his responsibilities under the lease to the new landlord just as he would have done with the old landlord. In a tenancy at will, however, the tenant has no such protection. Such tenancies terminate automatically, regardless of the intention of the parties, upon the sale of the property to a new owner. The new landlord, of course, is free to create new tenancy-at-will relationships with existing tenants if he so desires.

Read the lease carefully before you sign it. Most lawyers would rather check a lease for problems before you sign it, and negotiate new terms if necessary, than fight about it later in court. Moreover, the time it takes an attorney to warn of potential problems is usually much less—and less expensive— than court time later.

Read the entire lease, even the small print. Anything you find confusing should be clarified. Handwritten changes on a standard lease form are usually valid when initialed by both landlord and tenant. On the other hand, verbal agreements (such as waiving a prohibition against pets) are often not enforceable.

Try to get the landlord to agree to change standard clauses, such as those which obligate the tenant to make repairs or which unreasonably regulate the tenant's conduct (by, for example, forbidding pets or specifying hours after which a stereo cannot be played). If you might be transferred to another area by your employer, try to make the lease flexible by having the landlord agree to give you the right to sublet, subject to the landlord's "reasonable refusal to withhold his consent." You should insist that your security deposit be placed in an interest-bearing account (as many states require) and that the total is returned to you at the end of the lease if you live up to all your promises.

Both landlord and tenant have rights. The landlord has the right to receive rent, to enter the premises for necessary repairs, and to recover the premises at the end of the term of the lease in the same general condition as existed when the tenant moved in (allowing for normal wear and tear).

Tenants have the right to use the premises, undisturbed, for the purposes for which they were rented, to have at least the common areas kept in good repair by the landlord, and to recover their security deposit if they have not breached the lease.

Most of the following terms are found in the typical residential lease, although sometimes you must look hard to find them.

1. The full names of the landlord and tenant
2. The address of the property
3. The amount of rent, and details as to when it becomes due (either weekly, monthly, or yearly) and on what day of the month or week
4. Information as to which utilities, if any, are to be paid for, and provided by, the landlord, and which are to be the responsibilities of the tenant
5. The term of the lease and the expiration date (in the

case of a tenancy for years), or the period of the lease
(in a periodic tenancy)

6. The amount and method of notice to be given prior to
   terminating a periodic tenancy
7. The purpose for which the property has been leased
   (e.g., residential, office, or commercial)
8. The rights and obligations of both the landlord and the
   tenant regarding repairs
9. The amount of any security deposit, the conditions upon
   which it is to be retained by the landlord rather than
   returned to the tenant, and whether it bears (and who
   is entitled to) interest
10. The rights, if any, of the tenant to assign or sublease
    the premises
11. The signatures of both landlord and tenant(s)

Commercial leases are generally much more complicated and
probably should be drafted by an experienced real-estate attorney.

The tenant is generally responsible for repairs. Absent an express written promise (which many modern leases contain),
the landlord historically has been under no duty to repair
leased premises. There were various common-law exceptions to
this rule: common areas (which are under the control of the
landlord), and hidden defects (unless the landlord pointed
them out to the tenant prior to the lease). In short, the tenant
is responsible for all repairs in the premises unless the landlord promises otherwise.

A few states have enacted (or adopted pursuant to court
rulings) an *implied warranty of habitability*. This standard is
often defined in terms of meeting the important requirements
of the local housing code. If the landlord won't fix them, tenants should report possible violations of the local housing code
to the proper authorities. If the property falls short of meeting
such warranty, the tenant's rent may be reduced by a court to
pay for repairs. Most states have specific statutes which forbid

landlords from attempting to evict tenants simply because they have reported violations to the authorities.

You may be able to move out prior to the expiration date in a tenancy for years. First, carefully read the lease: some leases allow for early termination if a tenant is transferred to another location by his or her employer.

Second, examine the lease for any restriction of your rights to assign or sublease the premises. An assignment means that another party could move in and become completely responsible for carrying out the obligations of your lease until the expiration date. A sublease means that you are still primarily responsible to the landlord, and that if the sublessee doesn't perform one of his duties (like paying the rent on time), the landlord can still sue you.

No matter what the lease says regarding your rights of assignment and sublease, if you want to get out of your lease, ask your landlord. Offer to find a replacement tenant. The landlord may let you out of the lease if he thinks he can get more rent from someone else or if he's tired of hearing you complain, for example, about the lack of heat. If there is no restriction in the lease, you have the legal right as a tenant to assign or sublease your interest in the property to another person. But the landlord may actually prefer to find his own substitute tenant—and his doing so makes life much simpler for you.

Unfortunately, most modern leases contain a restriction on the tenant's right to sublease or assign. If your lease does contain such a restriction, and your landlord does not agree to waive it, your rights are limited. At common law, a tenant was responsible to pay rent to the landlord for the entire term of a tenancy for years—whether or not the premises were occupied. The landlord could refuse to let the tenant assign or sublease his interest to another person, and still sue the original tenant for the entire amount of rent. Most states, however, now have laws obligating the landlord in such situations to *mitigate damages*—that is, to make a reasonable attempt to find another tenant. But if the landlord makes reasonable, good-faith attempts to find another tenant and is unsuccessful, the original tenant is still legally responsible for the rent until expiration of the lease. (Likewise, if the landlord can find a substitute tenant, but only at a reduced rent, the old tenant is liable for the difference between the reduced rent and the original rent.) If your landlord claims to be unable to find a suitable substitute tenant, you should try to find a suitable substitute yourself —even if your lease forbids assignments or subleases. Be sure to explain to potential tenants that their tenancy is subject to the landlord's final approval (a requirement in most leases). Most courts would find the landlord to be acting unreasonably if he would refuse to accept a suitable tenant, and would release you from your obligation to pay future rent. But it's better to put a clause in the lease forbidding the landlord from *unreasonably refusing* to accept your subtenant.

New York law is different. If you're a tenant in New York City, see John Striker and Andrew Shapiro, *Super Tenant: New York City Tenant Handbook* (New York: Holt, Rinehart & Winston, 1978).

You may not have to pay anything if you are moving out of the premises prior to the expiration of your lease because of unlivable conditions. If your premises have become unbearable for some reason for which you aren't responsible, and the landlord has failed to make repairs within a reasonable time of being notified about the condition, the law recognizes a doctrine known as *constructive eviction*. That is, if you abandon the property because you found it to have become uninhabitable—there's no heat in the winter, or there's a large hole in the roof—a court might well consider your lease terminated by the landlord's own inaction. The important thing is to keep the potential court suit in mind before moving out: send certified letters to the landlord regarding the immediate need of repairs, and, where possible, take photographs. These provide documentary evidence to the court that the premises were indeed unlivable, and that it was the landlord and not you who acted unreasonably.

There are steps to be taken when leased premises need repairs. If the landlord has expressly promised to make necessary repairs, or the repairs are needed in a common area under the control of the landlord, your first step should be to telephone the landlord under the expectation that he will make the repairs promptly and thoroughly. If the landlord fails to take action in a reasonable period of time (from hours to ten working days, depending upon the nature of the repair), of course, send a certified letter to the landlord explaining the nature of the problem needing attention, and politely reminding him of his duty to repair. A certified letter indicates that the tenant means business and is preparing a court case. If the landlord continues to be recalcitrant, you might want to make the necessary repairs yourself, or have someone do them at your expense. In this situation it would be wise for you to take photographs, get a couple of estimates before hiring the repairman, and take any other measures that would assure a court of the reasonableness of your actions when you sue the landlord for reimbursement.

Failure to pay rent can lead to eviction. While withholding rent may seem to be the obvious way for the tenant to be compensated for making repairs, it could lead to eventual eviction. Because of a peculiarity of landlord-tenant law, the tenant's promise to pay rent and the landlord's promise to make repairs have always been considered by the law to be separate and independent. That is, the landlord's failure to make needed repairs has not been held in and of itself to be sufficient reason to excuse the tenant from the promise to make rent payments.

Thus, the best way for the tenant to be reimbursed for making necessary repairs is either a suit against the landlord in small-claims court, or the use of the rent-escrow procedure (described below) in areas where it is available.

Rent escrow is designed to help the tenant. It varies from state to state, but characteristically, rent escrow is a procedure where the tenant asks the court to establish an *escrow account* —one administered independently, out of reach of the landlord—because the premises have serious defects which the landlord refuses to correct.

A judge will listen to both sides before establishing an escrow account, and may decide to do any of the following: (a) terminate the lease, (b) dismiss the rent-escrow request, (c) order that the rent be reduced by a certain amount, or (d) order the establishment of a rent-escrow account.

Once an escrow account has been established, either the court, the landlord, or the tenant may request a second hearing. If the landlord can then show that the repairs have been made, the court will order that the rent be given to the landlord.

If the repairs are still not made after a period of time has elapsed, the court can (a) order that all or some of the money be given back to the tenant, the landlord, or a third party to make repairs, (b) appoint a special administrator to ensure that the repairs are made, and/or (c) order that some or all of the money in the account be given to the landlord to prevent foreclosure on the mortgage.

In some states, if the landlord still has not made a good-faith attempt to make the repairs after six months, the judge may order that the funds be given back to the tenant. However, the tenant is still obligated to pay future rent into the escrow account. If the tenant does not regularly pay the rent into the court's escrow account once it has been established, the court can order that any existing escrow funds be turned over to the landlord.

A landlord must take steps before evicting a tenant. When the lease expires in a tenancy with an express expiration date, and it is not renewed, the tenant must move out; no notice is required from the landlord. If the tenant has breached some important term of the lease (such as failure to pay the rent when due), the landlord can consider the lease terminated before the expiration date, and require that the tenant move out after reasonable notice. Such notice should be clear and definite, delivered to the tenant directly; it should contain an express request that the tenant "quit the premises and deliver up possession" to the landlord before a certain date. If a tenant responds to the notice by paying the amount of rent due, and the landlord accepts payment, the landlord has abandoned the right to evict the tenant (unless and until the lease is breached again).

If the tenant fails either to pay the back rent or to move out of the premises, the landlord can begin legal eviction proceedings. The court clerk should be able to give forms and advice. The services of an attorney should not be needed in a simple "failure to pay rent" case. Payment of back rent at any time prior to an eviction warrant (which must be signed by a judge) will stop the eviction process. In any event, there can be no eviction without a court hearing.

Prepare for housing court the same way you would prepare for small-claims court. See Chapter 14.

A tenant should know about security deposits. It is perfectly legal and a common practice for landlords to require security deposits, but many states have laws designed to protect tenants from being defrauded by the landlord under the guise of such practice. For example, some states specify that the security deposit may not be more than two months' rent or $50.00, whichever is greater. The landlord must give the tenant a receipt for the security deposit, although it may be included as part of the lease.

If you ask for it, you are usually entitled by law to a written list of existing damages within fifteen days of the date you move in. This list protects you in case of a dispute over the property's condition when you move out—that is, from the possibility that the landlord will try to hold you liable for damages caused by a prior tenant. You should check the list carefully to be sure it is accurate and, most important, complete.

The tenant generally has the right to be present when the landlord inspects the property for damages at the end of the lease. Some state laws provide that the landlord may not keep any of the security deposit if he fails to inform the tenant of this right to be present during final inspection. In fact, many states have statutes which provide that a tenant is entitled to punitive damages should the landlord fail to tell him about his rights under state landlord-tenant laws.

Finally, many states require that landlords place security deposits in an interest-bearing savings account, the accumulated sum to be returned to the tenant within forty-five days of the tenant's vacating the premises. As a tenant, you should always insist upon that in the lease—it's only fair, and never illegal.

The landlord may be entitled to keep the security deposit. Unless the terms of the lease provide otherwise, the landlord is generally allowed to keep all or part of the deposit if the tenant leaves owing unpaid rent or having damaged the property beyond normal wear and tear. But if any portion of the security deposit is withheld for damages, the law in many states requires that the landlord write the tenant by certified mail within thirty days after he vacates the property, giving a list of damages claimed and a statement showing the cost of repairs. In these states, failure to send the tenant the written damages list within thirty days causes forfeit of the landlord's right to retain any of the security deposit regardless of damages.

Finally, a landlord may not charge a penalty for a tenant's breaking of the lease. Generally, even a tenant who breaks the lease or is evicted, can recover all or part of the security deposit by giving the landlord written notice within forty-five days after the move and including a forwarding address. As mentioned before, the landlord must send such a tenant a written list of damages within thirty days of the request for one, along with a statement showing the actual repair costs. The landlord may subtract the actual repair costs or lost rent from the security deposit, but must return the rest of the money due to the tenant.

Check to see if there's a tenants' association. A group of tenants can be much more effective than an individual in bringing to bear reasonable pressure upon a landlord to make needed improvements on the property or to keep rental fees within certain guidelines. If there is no tenants' association to which you can refer your problem before going to a lawyer, you might want to organize one. This can be accomplished in any number of ways, sometimes as easily as convening an informal meeting.

Certain kinds of discrimination in housing are illegal. Federal (and many state) laws prohibit a landlord from discriminating against a tenant because of race, religion, sex, age, or national origin. If you feel that such discrimination has occurred, contact your local housing authority or equal-opportunity commission.

Note, however, that in many areas landlords may discriminate against people with children, pets, unpopular hobbies, and the like.

3

Buying and Selling a House

Set thine house in order.
—ISAIAH 38:1

For most homeowners, their house is their most substantial investment—and buying or selling a house can be a traumatic experience. It need not be, though, especially when the typical transaction can be so easily understood.

You do not always need a real-estate agent or a lawyer when you buy or sell a house. Neither is absolutely necessary. If you are selling, you might decide that it's advantageous for you to sell the house yourself and pocket the commission an agent would normally take. If you are a buyer, you might not have such a choice: the house that you are interested in buying may already be "listed" by a real-estate agent. (If you should see a house before an agent is involved, ask the seller to have you specifically excluded from any subsequent agency agreement.)

A lawyer can be helpful with the contract. The most useful service a lawyer can perform for both buyer and seller is to review the sales contract *before* it is signed. The sales contract determines who pays various costs and what is to be sold along with the house. Your concern here is to create contract

24

terms in your best interest; once the agreement is signed, even the best lawyer can't help you. In some states, real-estate agents are allowed to create sales contracts (usually by filling in blanks on standard forms); in a few other states, this would be considered the unauthorized practice of law and is thus forbidden. (Check with your real-estate agent or with the bar association in your state.) But even if the agent can't create the contract for you, you can always do it yourself; the rules against unauthorized practice of law only prohibit acting on someone else's behalf.

An agent can be helpful. The major advantages to retaining an agent are that agents advertise, screen buyers, help set an attractive asking price, advise as to whether to accept a lower offer, and assist in arranging various kinds of financing.

The agent works for the seller. If you decide to sell your house through a real-estate agent, he or she will take a commission— a percentage of the selling price—as payment. An agent is familiar with the ins and outs of house selling, as well as the real-estate laws, and should know the market in your area for house selling (as well as where and how to get interested buyers). If you are a buyer, don't be misled by the friendliness of the agent; he or she is really the seller's agent, gets paid out of the proceeds of the sale, and is primarily interested in making a sale.

If you're a seller, your agent must work for you. The real-estate agent is responsible to you and not to the buyer (although, if your agent finds a buyer, he must operate in a fair manner toward both of you). The agent may be a solo practitioner working in your area or may be a member of a multistate or even national real-estate firm.

In either case, you (as the seller) contract with the agent, setting out the terms under which the agent will show and sell your house on the market. These terms include what type of listing you will have (explained below); how long the agent

will be allowed to show your house to buyers (anywhere between thirty and ninety days, with provisions for extensions if
mutually agreed upon); how much commission will be paid
(anywhere from 5 to 10 percent, depending on your location—
some markets bear a higher commission rate than others);
when that commission is payable (for example, if a ready,
willing, and able buyer is presented, or if a sale is actually
made, the latter being the more favorable term for the seller);
and any other terms that you or the agent feel are necessary to
be stated in your agreement.

If you're a buyer, the agent must treat you fairly. But you
should remember that an agent's primary responsibility is to
the seller. Buyers need not pay the agent any commission or
other fees; the agent gets paid a percentage of the proceeds of
selling the house. (On rare occasions, a buyer will contract
with a real-estate agent to find a house. In a market with fewer
sellers than buyers, this practice may occur more frequently.)
    An agent must treat a buyer fairly—that is, he cannot en-
gage in misrepresentation or any other unethical practice.
Likewise, you cannot be discriminated against on the basis of
your age, sex, race, color, or national origin.

Listing ageements take several forms. A house is listed when
the real-estate agent contracts with the seller to place it on the
market. The most favorable agreement to the real-estate agent
(and also the most common arrangement) is the *exclusive
right to sell* contract. Under this type of contract, the real-
estate agent you select is the only one who can sell your house,
and even if you produce the buyer without the help of the
agent, the agent gets a commission. In other words, no one else
has the right to sell your house during the time of the agency.
    Under an *open listing* arrangement, you contract with an
agent to sell your house for an agreed-upon commission, but
you retain the right to sell the house yourself *or* to engage the
services of another agent. This is the loosest type of arrangement, giving you the most flexibility and exposing the agent to

the greatest risk. Obviously, it is the least favored arrangement in the real-estate industry.

In any case, you should read the agency contract very carefully, to determine your rights and liabilities.

A *multiple listing* service is an agreement among the real-estate agents in an area to place the houses that they have contracted to sell on a master list which can be used by any participating agent. That is, the fees are split between the originally contracted agent and the one who actually finds a buyer. Agents who multiple-list have a much wider choice of houses to sell.

If you don't want a number of different agents showing your house, you may request that it not be placed on a multiple list. Your chances of finding a good buyer, however, are thereby diminished.

Commissions can be split. Even if your house is multiple-listed, your original agent will often be the one to show prospective buyers your house. If a buyer is brought to your agent's attention by an agent from another firm, the commission is split. Therefore, you do not have to pay any extra when another agent is involved in the sale.

Read your listing contract. Try to get the most flexibility in your listing contract. For example, try to have the agent allow you to sell your house independently if you can. (The agent will likely argue that your entry into the market will make it more difficult for him.)

At any rate, make sure that you have told the agent if there are any possible buyers with whom you have already made contact—and make sure that these buyers appear on the face of the listing contract as "excluded." This is your protection that, even in an otherwise exclusive listing, you will be able to sell your house to a previously known buyer without having to pay an agent's commission.

Another way of maintaining flexibility is to contract for short periods of time with the agent. For example, you might agree

to an exclusive listing for thirty to sixty days, and then open up
the listing for other agents. You can always agree to extensions
of the listing contract. Agreeing to representation for short
periods of time will make the agent more likely to concentrate
on selling your house faster.

*The main thing to remember is that, as with any other
agreement (including the sales contract), all the terms in a
listing contract are negotiable. This is true even if the terms
are already spelled out on a printed form.*

Make certain to read the listing contract carefully. (You may
be agreeing to pay an agent who produces a ready, willing,
and able buyer even if the deal eventually falls through.) Also,
don't be afraid to shop around for the real-estate agent with
the best terms and commission rates. Speak to several agents in
your area before listing your house.

Commissions are negotiable. Commissions usually run from 5
to 10 percent of the sale price. Be certain you agree on the
commission.

If you have listed your house under an exclusive listing, you
will owe the agent a commission if your house is sold during
the time of the contract (or within a reasonable time after the
contract has expired, if the ultimate buyer was presented during the contract terms or any extensions). Don't think that
because the contract has expired, you can sell your house to a
buyer introduced by the agent without paying the agent's
commission. Of course, if the house is sold to a buyer excluded
by name in the listing contract, you need pay no commission.

**The contract of sale is critical to the transaction, for both
buyer and seller.** If you are listing your house with a real-estate
agent, the agent will have a contract of sale for you and the
buyer to sign. If you are selling your house without the aid of
an agent, you can use a form contract for the sale of real estate
(which is usually available from stationery or legal-supply
stores).

The sales contract is a binding agreement between you and

the buyer, setting out the terms under which the buyer will make the purchase. These terms include the settlement date for the property—when the transfer will be made (usually thirty to ninety days from the signing of the sales contract)—and the terms that the buyer and the seller want and agree to. It is the single most important document in any sale of property. Read it very carefully. If you have only enough money to pay a lawyer for one service, have him review the sales contract—before you sign.

All terms in the sales contract are fully negotiable. In other words, try to make the best deal possible.

As a seller, you might ask for some good-faith money to be paid at the signing of the contract, and assurances that you will be paid in full at the time of settlement. As a buyer, you might want to specify that you have the right to choose the title-insurance company or attorney who will make sure there are no outstanding claims against your house. (The title-insurance company that made the title search when the seller originally bought the house will generally give a better rate for such a search now.)

Both parties will want to set a convenient settlement date. If you are a seller moving to another house or an apartment, be sure that you won't have to move out of your present house before the new one is ready. You can protect yourself by providing in the contract that you will be able to rent your old house from the new owners, which will allow you to stay in the house as long as you need to.

Specify what extras come with the house—drapes, carpets, appliances, etc.—so there are no misunderstandings later. If you are planning to take your washer and dryer with you, for example, state your intentions.

As a buyer, you have the same right as the seller to make the best deal possible in the sales contract. You certainly would want the contract to be contingent on your getting acceptable financing for the house. This means that the contract will be terminated if you cannot find the financing specified in the contract. (For example, if the contract specified a 14 percent, thirty-year mortgage, it would not be enforceable if you were unable to get such financing within a designated time period.) Allow enough time to get the financing you seek. If the mortgage that the seller has is assumable and you choose to assume it, specify the following terms: that you are entitled to the interest on the money deposited to secure the transaction; that the maximum damages for a breach will be forfeiture of the deposit; and that you have the right to choose both lawyer and title company.

You might also want to make the contract contingent on the house passing a termite or roofing inspection. This type of term will protect you if the house is damaged in a way not noticeable to you. If the house fails to pass any inspections that you specify, you would not be obligated to purchase it. If the house has well water, you might specify in the contract that the house pass a specific test that measures the amount of water in reserve. Contact a local surveyor or the county water office for information on such tests.

Finally, make sure that you know what covenants and easements exist on the property. *Covenants* are agreements between the previous owners of the house that all the owners in the neighborhood agree to. These are the by-laws of the neighborhood and, although you were not party to their acceptance, they are binding on all subsequent and present houseowners in the area. A covenant may restrict, for example, where garages or other buildings may be built, or set up binding rules such as how often houses must be painted and grass trimmed.

Easements are rights that other people may have in your property. Some may be written, but some may arise through continued use (or may be otherwise implied by the law). For example, the electric company may have an easement to run power lines over your property. Other easements may not be so benign: a neighbor might have an easement (purchased from a prior owner or by operation of law) to drive his car over your property to get to his property. Easements which concern your property and your neighbor's are said to "run with the land"—that is, they exist no matter who owns the house. Be sure you know what you are buying.

Inspections are sometimes required by law. Many states require that the seller of a house pay for inspections—for example, for termites—and repair or correct certain kinds of deficiencies.

An escrow agreement brings in a third party. An escrow agreement is sometimes made in the sales contract; it appoints a neutral third party to handle the transactions at closing (settlement). An escrow agent is generally appointed by the buyer; he is sometimes a member of the title-insurance company, a representative of a lending institution, or an independent third party (such as an attorney). Houses financed through FHA or VA mortgages (discussed below) must be handled through escrow agents.

The escrow agent will handle much of the paperwork involved, make the necessary apportions of cost between the buyer and seller, and make sure the moneys go to the right places. He is the stakes holder who keeps the money during the closing transactions in order to make sure the right parties get what they have contracted for. The escrow agent takes the sales contract and, applying its terms, lists what charges are payable by the seller and the buyer. If there are unpaid real-estate taxes, he makes the division—prorating it for the amount of time during the year the seller owned the house. (For example, if the seller owned the house from January to June, each party would be responsible for half the real-estate taxes for that year.) The same divisions are made for utility bills and the like. The escrow agent makes sure that the lender pays the amount he has contracted to pay, and that the seller gets what he or she is entitled to under the contract after the necessary deductions listed on the settlement sheet (such as the commission payable to a real-estate agent, the document taxes, etc.). Credits are made for payments already tendered.

There may also be an agreement under escrow that certain
funds are to be withheld from the seller until he has performed
a promised function, such as painting specified parts of the
house or repairing a driveway.

A settlement sheet reflects the sales contract. Under federal
law, a settlement sheet must be prepared on a form printed
by the Department of Housing and Urban Development.
There are two columns, listing the respective costs to be borne
by the seller and the buyer. These terms are generally negotiable, but they usually work as follows:

Transfer taxes are generally divided equally by the seller
and buyer, as are the *escrow* costs. The buyer is usually responsible for any *appraisals* necessary because of the loan or
local law, and for the *points* payable to the lender (see section
on mortgages, below; FHA or VA loans do not allow buyers
to be charged in excess of one point). The buyer also pays the
legal fees if any, as well as for a *report on his credit rating.*

The seller is usually responsible for *commissions* on the sale
of the house, *document stamps* necessary for the deed of sale
to be recorded in the local county or state office (see below),
notary fees for signatures on the deeds, and *mortgage payments that are in arrears.*

Although the above division of costs is the normal practice,
remember that all these fees are negotiable and may be divided differently at the time of the sales contract (or at the
time of the escrow agreement).

Title insurance guarantees a buyer's deed. Title insurance is
simply an insurance policy that is purchased from a company
that has searched the records in the county or state office of
land records and has determined that the previous owners
have not made any transactions or done any other thing that
has placed on your new house a *lien* or other *encumbrance*—a
form of debt that must be paid before the house can be transferred to a new owner free and clear.

If the title-insurance company has found no encumbrances

on title property, the title is said to be "free and clear of all clouds on the title," or merchantable, and it can be sold to the new buyer.

If an encumbrance is found, the present owner is usually responsible to pay it off before the property can be transferred.

Like any other insurance policy, a title-insurance policy protects buyers against a future happening. The title insurer has warranted to you that there are no encumbrances on the property; if any are later found, the insurer will pay them off (so long as you were not responsible). This protection lasts for the period you own the house and will further protect you should you want to sell your house later on.

Title to property should always be verified. You can do it yourself (with the help of the records-office clerk), or you can pay someone to have it done.

Although title insurance is not always required, it is a small investment against what later might be a big bill. Keep in mind that most lenders require title insurance (or the opinion of a lawyer that there are no encumbrances) before giving a mortgage.

There are different kinds of mortgages. Before you even sign the sales contract, it is a good idea to know the mortgage market in your area. You can't start too soon looking for possible means of financing.

Three basic types of financing are available.

Conventional mortgages come from commercial banks, savings and loan institutions, or mortgage brokers. Check with your family bank or other lending institutions in your area to find out what they are willing to lend you for the purchase of a house. A conventional loan charges interest based on the market rate, which is usually a percent or so over the prime rate (that which the bank charges its most favored customers). The buyer/borrower is usually required to pay for title insurance. Also, the bank will probably charge you *points* (or *document processing fees*). Points are several percentage points of the amount loaned (the number varies from bank to bank).

For example, if you are borrowing $100,000 and the bank is charging you 7 points as a loan origination fee, it is getting $7,000 just for making the loan. Although this is not part of the loan, it can greatly affect the amount you end up paying for a house. Points, like interest charges, are tax-deductible if they are not in the nature of a service fee, if they are for a mortgage on the buyer's principal residence, and if they are generally charged in your geographical area.

Federal Housing Administration loans are financed through banks or mortgage brokers, but are actually regulated by the Department of Housing and Urban Development. Such loans allow for a very small down payment; anyone is eligible. Lenders can finance up to the appraised value of the house, or up to a ceiling applicable to the local housing market. Because the FHA insures the loans (very acceptable to the lending institution), they can be for a long period of time and there is no prepayment penalty. FHA loans can be obtained only on houses that have been FHA-inspected, and amounts are determined according to local housing costs. The loan may not be approved until repairs are made pursuant to that inspection. Also, FHA lending institutions are limited to charging fewer points to the buyer; no regulations prohibit the assessing of points to the seller. (For further information about FHA loans, contact your local office of the Federal Housing Administration.)

Loans which are regulated by the *Veterans Administration* are also attractive, if you qualify. You must be an eligible veteran of the armed forces. Although VA loans are also made through commercial banks, a better than market rate is offered because the federal government guarantees a certain part of the loans in case of default (that is, if you are unable to make loan payments). VA loans are more easily assumable than FHA mortgages, and the period of time for payment is longer than those in conventional loans.

But there is also no limitation on points and interest the bank can charge the buyer. A VA appraisal is also necessary. (For more information about VA loans, and especially for the eligibility requirements, contact your local office of the Veterans Administration.)

In recent years, various forms of "creative financing" have been developed, including balloon mortgages and variable rate mortgages. *Balloon mortgages* are those under which only the interest is due during the term of the mortgage, with the entire principle due at the end of the term (which is usually short). *Variable rate mortgages* are those which reflect the prevailing interest rates; in other words, they fluctuate over time. Because they are so risky, you should not sign one unless there is an absolute ceiling of some kind.

A buyer should be assured of his mortgage rate. Lenders (*mortgagees*) are required by federal law to give each borrower, or *mortgagor*, a truth-in-lending statement. It shows the mortgagor exactly what rate he is paying on the mortgage, how much each payment will be—and what the total, ultimate cost of the purchase will be.

Remember that the higher the down payment (the amount that is not financed), the lower the ultimate cost of your purchase. In order to make an informed decision, ask the lender to explain (fully and clearly) the various mortgage plans available. Do not sign anything before you are absolutely certain you understand the terms.

There are other ways to finance the purchase of a house. You can assume the mortgage of the current owners, *if* the mortgage is assumable under its terms and the current mortgagor agrees. Obviously, lenders are not enthusiastic about letting a purchaser assume a 6 percent mortgage when the current rates are much higher. But a bank may be amenable to *blending* a mortgage rate—taking an average annual percentage rate between the old mortgage and the newer rates. Banks do like to attract and keep customers. Don't be intimidated.

You can lose your house if you default. If you default under a mortgage, the lender has the power to take your house from you. The mortgage is an agreement between you and the lender that, even though the house is titled in your name and you own the property, it is still subject to the lender's being paid. A deed of trust is often just another name for a mortgage, except that in some states the property is actually titled in the name of the bank; when you have finally paid off the house payments, the deed will be transferred to your name. A deed of trust is an easy way for a lender to establish an interest in your house, without a formal foreclosure and retitling procedure after a default. Make sure you know the options legally available in your state.

A bank does not always have to be involved in a mortgage. You may be able to arrange a private mortgage (through a well-heeled friend or relative) and avoid the hassles of dealing with a bank. The terms of the loan can be more flexible than those in a standard bank mortgage (or precisely the same, if both parties agree). As in any contract, everything is negotiable. It's probably a good idea to have a lawyer review the terms of a privately arranged financing agreement.

The settlement date must be agreed upon. The settlement date is the day specified in the sales contract that the final transactions will occur—the day you will have to make your down payment and the lender will have to present a check for the balance. (Some contracts of sale fix a time by which the settlement must take place, and the parties still have to agree on the actual time, date, and place.) At that time the seller will sign a deed over to you (or the mortgagee in a deed of trust) and the costs are allocated and paid.

If you understand what you've read so far, a lawyer for settlement probably isn't needed. Often a lawyer merely runs through a check list at the settlement, and pockets a hefty fee—usually a percentage of the purchase price—for his minimal efforts.

Banks frequently require their own lawyer at settlement of

houses they are financing—and charge the buyer for his services. See if you can persuade the bank to waive this requirement. Be an effective bargainer.

Of course, in a complicated property transaction (*not* the usual buying and selling of a one-family dwelling), lawyers can be very helpful.

The deed and the mortgage must be filed. Both the deed and the mortgage must be filed with the property records in your county or state (depending on the local law). This step is required so that you have a good claim to your property, and the seller cannot do anything further (such as sell it again or make loans against it). Check with your state or county government to see what you must do (and what costs you must pay) before the records can be filed.

If you have any questions, the clerk at the filing office can help you. If an escrow agent is present at the settlement, he will usually file the documents for you—especially if the agent is the title-insurance company.

There are federal tax consequences in selling a house. You should see a lawyer or an accountant if you are uncertain about them. Under current federal law, if you sell a house and do not buy another one for more than two years, you will be taxed on the entire amount of the gain from the sale; if you purchase another house within two years, you will be taxed only on that portion of the price of your old house which was not invested in your new house.

Buying a condominium is about the same as buying a house. Most states apply the same basic law to condominiums as to regular houses, in all stages of the purchase proceedings. Check with your local government's housing office for the rules in your area.

Financing a cooperative apartment is sometimes easier. Co-operatives (co-ops) are generally formed for the purpose of acquiring property. The shareholders are also lessees of the property; their shares are inseparable from the leases. Co-ops are usually corporations. Leases are usually long-term (e.g., ninety-nine years and renewable).

Financing a cooperative apartment is sometimes easier because more commercial money at better rates is available for purchasing a whole building (as opposed to individual units). The entire property can be subject to one mortgage. Owners of units in a cooperative have the same tax benefits as owners of private homes or condominiums.

Cooperatives are managed by boards of directors who are responsible for maintenance of all the property. Because of the amount of money usually involved in buying into a co-op, you should probably contact a lawyer (at least to review the transaction on paper).

4

Defective Products

Let the buyer beware.

           —Anonymous Latin proverb

ALL too often, we buy products that don't work when we open up the box or that work for a while and then stop. Perseverance, common sense, and a willingness to complain can often do as much for you as a lawyer in getting your money back, a replacement, or having repairs done at someone else's expense. Remember, most stores want your business in the future and are willing to try to "work things out" to see that you are satisfied. But you are more likely to succeed if you know your rights, even if it's not worth your time and trouble to sue the department store over a ball-point pen with no ink or a mouse trap with no spring.

All products have warranties. Warranties on almost every product are provided by federal and state laws. Some commercial code is in force in every state and the District of Columbia. It usually covers *goods*—products that can be moved at the time of purchase. In addition, there are several federal statutes which help protect consumers from defective products.

Under the Uniform Commercial Code, which has been

adopted in some form or another by almost every state, warranties are generally classified as either *express* or *implied*.

Know what warranties mean. Implied warranties automatically come with the product, regardless of any actions by the purchaser or the salesperson. Even if there is no written warranty, the law implies one. Two of the most common implied warranties are the implied warranty of merchantability and the implied warranty of fitness for a particular purpose.

An *implied warranty of merchantability* covers *goods* (such as appliances or cars—things movable at the time of sale—but not houses or plots of land) that are bought from *merchants* (people who are usually in the business of selling such goods). For example, an automobile dealer is usually in the business of selling cars; he is not a merchant with respect to the desk he might want to sell from his office.

The goods are *merchantable* if they can "pass without objection in the trade." This means that the product must be as good as similar products sold by other merchants. For example, the wood you want to buy from a lumberyard must be of the same quality sold by other lumber yards in your area. The product must also be "fit for the ordinary purpose for which such goods are used." A barbecue grill, for example, must be sturdy enough to hold enough charcoal for cooking. Additionally, the product must live up to any promises made on the package or in the literature included with it.

An *implied warranty of fitness for a particular purpose* arises when you tell the salesperson the purpose for which you need the product, or when the salesperson has reason to know how you are going to use it. If you are clearly relying on the salesperson's judgment and skill in selecting a product, an implied warranty of fitness for a particular purpose has been created. For example, if you told a salesperson at a paint store that you needed paint to cover a certain kind of masonry, his suggestion of a particular paint would carry with it an implied warranty that it is the proper paint for that application. If you are buying an automobile, and you tell the salesperson that you intend to tow a trailer with that car, a warranty is created that the car is suitable to pull a trailer.

Express warranties are created when the salesperson or manufacturer of a product has stated or demonstrated to you a quality or characteristic of the product. And you buy the product because of that statement or promise. If the salesperson tells you that the radio he is selling is a stereo, and it is not, he has breached an express warranty.

An express warranty may also arise when the salesperson shows you any models or samples and you buy the product because of these models or samples. For example, if you were buying storm doors for your home because you liked the sample which you were shown, the seller has breached an express warranty if the doors don't work properly.

Warranties that are written and come with a product are also express warranties—and they must conform to federal law. The federal Magnuson-Moss Warranty Act states that a warranty on a product, if one is made, must be labeled as either a Full Warranty or a Limited Warranty. The difference between the two rests in the remedies available to the consumer and in the amount of time during which the consumer can claim damages under the warranty. A full warranty obviously provides more protection.

Warranties protect the manufacturer as well. It is important to remember that warranties are often designed more to protect the manufacturer—that is, to limit his liability—than to protect the consumer. Artfully worded warranties give the opposite impression. Nevertheless, comparing warranties enables the careful shopper to choose wisely among similar products. One product may be covered under a warranty more comprehensive or more long-lasting than another. Under federal law, you have the right to ask the salesperson to show you a product's warranty before you buy it.

Services are usually not covered by warranties. But you are still protected by law for services that are inadequate. Services

provided by professionals are regulated by various state
boards. Although there is no "implied warranty," practitioners
must conform to standards of conduct and their regulatory
boards can assist in determining whether there has been a
violation of these standards. Besides doctors and lawyers,
many different professionals are licensed by state boards:
home-improvement contractors, veterinarians, morticians,
mechanics, real-estate brokers, even landscapers may be licensed by state boards. Check with your state or county
government to locate the board that regulates the service provider against whom you have a complaint. Even if the service
provider is not subject to agency regulation, at the very least,
he is still obligated to perform his services in a workmanlike
manner, and do what he says he will do. If he doesn't, contact
the consumer protection agency in your state or local government.

Be reasonable and use common sense. As with any dispute
between people, your first step should be to let the seller or
service provider know that you are dissatisfied with the
product or service. Many businesspeople will go out of their
way to correct your problem, even if they think that they are
right. Dissatisfied customers are bad business.

If products are involved, return them to the store as soon as
possible after you discover the defect, and ask for a refund or
an exchange. Many stores will cooperate, because they too can
return the product (to the manufacturer) for a refund. Many
sellers need authorization from the manufacturer to return the
goods; if this is the case, allow the businessperson enough time
to obtain such permission.

If a service is involved, invite the service provider to inspect
the work done. If you are dissatisfied with how a painter
painted your house, for example, invite him to inspect the
work and suggest how you can resolve your dispute.

Contact the manufacturer. If you find that you are still dissatisfied with a product, contact the manufacturer. This might

also be necessary if you have had the product for some period of time. The manufacturer's address should be found in any written warranty; otherwise, contact the store where you made the purchase. A growing number of manufacturers have toll-free telephone numbers which you can call for advice or to register a complaint. (To find a toll-free number, call the operator at 1-800-555-1212.) Where automobiles are involved and the dealer is not cooperative, contact the manufacturer's area sales or service representative. In most cases, you will be asked to put your complaint in writing—a good practice anyway, so that all the facts about the grievance will be on record.

If you have not gotten any cooperation from a service provider who is a member of a national or regional chain (such as a franchised auto or transmission repair shop), contact the chain's main office. Your state's Department of Motor Vehicles can also help with automobile warranty problems.

Withhold payment for a defective product or poor service. In many cases you'd be wise to withhold payment. Here is a good application of the old rubric "possession is nine tenths of the law." If you keep the money, the burden is on someone else to prove a case. You should be certain, however, that the manufacturer knows why you are withholding payments, and that he may be entitled to take back the product. If you paid by credit card, notify the credit-card company not to pay that seller or service provider (ask your credit-card company for the proper procedure).

The general rule is that you are not obligated to pay for products or services that are inadequate. For example, if you have purchased a toaster that will not toast, you have complained to the merchant who sold it to you, and he has refused to do anything about your complaint, then you should withhold your payment. You will usually get fast results. Similarly, if you have made a purchase with a credit card, notify the credit-card company of your complaint and (using the procedures prescribed) ask that all your other payments be made except the one in dispute. This is your right under the federal Truth in Lending Act—provided that the product or service cost more than $50 and that it was bought in your home state or within a hundred miles of your home.

It's often difficult to get your money back. You are in a more difficult position if you have already paid. You may reject those goods on their delivery to you, or within a reasonable time you may "revoke your acceptance" of the goods. For an effective rejection, you must notify the seller of your rejection and not use the product. If you have accepted the goods by not rejecting them when they were delivered, or have used them for a period of time, you may still revoke your acceptance of the product if the defect impairs its value to you.

There are technical aspects of these questions, however, which can better be answered by your state or local consumer-protection bureau. If in your judgment a substantial sum of money is involved, contact a lawyer.

Go to court as a last resort. If all else fails, you can bring an action in court for the price of the product or service, and any other damages that have resulted from the inadequacy (such as if you had to buy a replacement item because the one you originally bought was so defective as to render it useless). You can pursue these remedies in a small-claims court if the amount in controversy is small enough. (See Chapter 14.)

If you go to court, you are not limited to a refund of the purchase price. You might also claim consequential and incidental damages.

Consequential damages are damages that occur as a result of a warranty breach. For example, if your car has been improperly serviced and you need a car for work, you might be able to rent one and collect from the service provider the cost of rental.

Incidental damages are those that occur more directly because of the breach. For example, if your car needs to be towed back to the shop because of faulty repairs, the towing charges could be claimed as incidental damages.

Warranties sometimes apply to used goods. A manufacturer's express warranty may have expired or may be applicable only to the first purchaser. You do not have any implied warranties against someone who is not a merchant dealing in such goods. And even if the product is covered by an implied warranty from the manufacturer, you may have only a limited period of time in which to bring a warranty claim. (Some states allow four years or more after the product was sold to the original owner; other states have no such time limit.)

Many states require a used-car dealer to offer at least a minimum warranty, such as ninety days or six months. If in doubt, contact your state's department of transportation. (Even with used cars, you might still be able to purchase an express warranty. Check with several dealers in your area.)

Caveat emptor—**Be a wise shopper.** Besides comparing warranties, you should shop for the most reliable manufacturer. If the product is expensive or complicated, make sure you feel confident that the manufacturer will still be around if you need parts or services later on. Studebaker and Hudson parts are not easy to come by. Be an informed consumer. Ask other people who have similar products how well they work. Read magazines that test common consumer goods, such as *Consumer Reports*.

You should also educate yourself about the product by testing it yourself. If you are purchasing a car, drive it before you buy. If you are purchasing a vacuum cleaner, ask the sales person for a demonstration. Don't be afraid to ask questions. Be firm (without being offensive) when dealing with salespeople. Do not let them act as if they are doing you a favor by selling you something.

There is probably a consumer-protection agency in your state. Look in your telephone directory under state government.

When there's an injury, see a lawyer. If the injury is serious you'd probably be wise to contact a lawyer and explain the problem to him. The same is true for any substantial damage to your property.

5

Debtors' and Creditors' Rights and Obligations

Creditors have better memories than debtors.
—Benjamin Franklin
POOR RICHARD'S ALMANACK

Eᴀᴄʜ year, countless consumers get into trouble over their debts. While no one can teach you how to manage a Cadillac life style on a Chevy income, if you, the debtor, understand the facts about credit, life can be much easier for you.

Not surprisingly, credit begins with a contract. Thus, the debts that you incur are your own doing and almost always result from a contract that you have signed. This takes us back to the principal point of Chapter 1: if you don't like the terms of a contract—including the one that obligates you to pay 18 percent interest per month on your average outstanding balance—don't sign it.

In fact, credit contracts give you not only one chance to avoid problems but several. Just because you have a credit card or a charge account from your local department store doesn't mean that you have to use them or that you are forbidden to pay the whole bill when it comes in the mail. And, as we will see later, there are various laws that protect debtors from themselves and require creditors to make certain disclosures to insure that borrowers truly understand what they are getting themselves into.

Credit plans vary in their complexity and value. Most credit cards are maintained by banks and large merchants, which hope that consumers will make purchases beyond their immediate means and will thus borrow money at high rates of interest. If you have an account with a store, you may be extended credit without interest being charged. There are *revolving accounts* (where you must make monthly payment but can still buy items on credit on that account), and *closed-end accounts* (where you make a specific purchase or borrow a certain amount of money on credit, and you cannot borrow any more on that account until you have paid off that amount).

You need a few pieces of basic information in order to make intelligent decisions relating to credit transactions:

1. *Amounts.* Before you make any credit purchases, it is a good idea to know exactly how much you may be borrowing. If a store is handling the financing of your transaction, ask what the maximum cost to you could be.
2. *Terms.* Once you have signed a credit contract, even if you did not pay attention to figures, you are obliged to pay according to the terms of the agreement. There might be a lump-sum payment at the end of a specified time, or several monthly payments. In revolving credit accounts, the amounts may vary. Interest rates, of course, are very important. Do not be fooled by lenders (merchants) who state they are not charging you interest. Rest assured that, except for the thirty days' grace period generally granted in standard billing, interest charges are hidden somewhere in the price. By saying he is not charging

interest, a merchant is often trying to circumvent disclosure laws. Be assertive. Ask to compare the amount you'd ultimately pay under maximum interest charges with what the item in question would cost if you paid cash on the spot. Remember that interest rates must somewhere be stated in terms of annual percentages. Much more often than not, you will be paying the highest rate allowed by the law of your state.

3. *Collateral.* You should make certain you know exactly what collateral you may be putting up for a loan. Collateral is what you promise to sacrifice to the lender if you fail to make your payments. Some small-loan companies make you put up as collateral personal possessions that are worth several times the amount of the loan. Credit-card companies generally do not ask for any collateral, but may attach the accounts you have in their banks. Remember, collateral can be used only to provide repayment of the debt (plus interest). The rest goes back to the borrower.

4. *Default procedures.* At the time of the transaction, find out what the lender will do if you default on your loan or credit purchase. Lenders have different ways of dealing with this situation.

Under both federal and state truth-in-lending statutes, the creditor must make this information available to you in a written statement prior to your signing any financing agreement. Unfortunately, few consumers bother to read this piece of paper, and those who do often find it incomprehensible. It's frequently easier (and safer) to ask the lender to explain the terms in plain English. If there are additional charges (for insurance, for example), these too must be stated in the disclosure statement.

A lender (whether bank, merchant, or loan company) who does not give you the required disclosure statement, can be subject to criminal penalties brought by the Federal Trade

Commission or your state credit commissioner, as well as to civil penalties brought by you as an aggrieved debtor.

Most states limit the rate of interest a lender is allowed to charge. If a higher rate is applied, the lender is guilty of *usury.* Usurious loans are illegal and unenforceable.

Under the federal truth-in-lending laws, banks and other lenders are required to state clearly their rates of interest— which in more cases than not are at the legal maximums.

Call your local banking commissioner to determine the maximum rates allowed by your state.

The Rights of Creditors and Debtors

Much of commercial law is concerned with the collection of debts. Both federal and state laws set out various steps that can or cannot be taken with regard to debts owed. Many of these laws are designed to protect the rights of both the debtor and the creditor in these transactions.

Creditors. The law recognizes the right of a creditor to receive the money owed to him. If you are a creditor, your first step should be to notify the debtor that he owes you something. If he is recalcitrant, you can either continue negotiations, contact a debt-collection agency (which will probably take anywhere from 30 to 50 percent of the balance due), or go to court. (See Chapter 14.) There the object is to get the debt reduced to a judgment. (Once a judgment is rendered, the debt has been judicially recognized; you don't have to prove anything except that it hasn't been paid, and you also have a long time to collect—generally, twenty years.)

But even before a judgment is rendered in your favor, you must be careful about how you go about collecting your debt. Under federal and many state consumer-debt laws, you cannot use unfair, abusive, or illegal means to enforce your rights. You cannot call a debtor on the telephone at unreasonable hours, or contact the debtor's friends, neighbors, or even relatives about the debt. You may not use foul or abusive language—nor any pieces of paper that appear as if they are issued by courts when they are really not. Nor can you threaten criminal actions if the only reason you are doing so is to collect the debt. Any actions that you take that are unlawful may subject you to more liability than the debt is worth.

(Generally, the state laws afford debtors greater protection. Federal statutes cover less than 2 percent of the debts collected in the nation, while state laws regulate a wider assortment of creditors and debt-collection organizations.)

Once a judgment is entered verifying that you are legally entitled to collect a debt, you have several options. If your agreement with the debtor mentioned an item as collateral for the credit extended, you are entitled to take the item pursuant to an attachment—a subsequent suit entered in a state court which would allow you to take such collateral. If your loan is not secured by collateral, you might ask for garnishment of the debtor's wages—that is, having the debtor's employer pay you directly out of the debtor's weekly pay check. Again, this action must be sought in court and approved by a judge. You may also try to get a lien on any property owned by the debtor. None of these procedures requires a lawyer. But because every state has different procedures and rules regarding attachments, forfeitures, and garnishments, ask the clerk of your local small-claims court. (See Chapter 14.)

Debtors. As a debtor, you have the right to be protected from abusive and unlawful behavior on the part of the lender or creditor. Under both federal and state debt-collection acts, you must be treated fairly. You are also entitled to "due process"— a fair application of the laws—when a creditor takes you to court to collect his debt. You have a right to answer: you may assert that you do not owe the money, or disagree with the amount the creditor says you owe, or feel you never received the benefit of the money or goods in question. Even if your loan was transferred from the original creditor from

whom you bought goods to someone else, you are entitled to
the same defenses.

If you have difficulty paying a debt, try to reach an arrangement with the creditor that is mutually satisfactory. If you can
prevent the creditor from taking you to court, you will avoid
later difficulties in garnishments, attachments, or forfeitures of
collateral. You might also consider asking the creditor for a
little time to get your finances in order—for example, through
a debt-consolidation loan available through your local bank or
finance company.

You might also get in touch with a debtor counseling service
run by your state or a local charitable organization.

Bankruptcy and Debt Adjustment

Under federal law, a person may apply for bankruptcy or for
debt adjustment when he feels that he is no longer able to
pay his debts. *Bankruptcy*, in the traditional sense, means a
complete discharge of a person's debts by means of collecting
those of his assets which are not protected under federal or
state law and distributing the proceeds to creditors.

Debt adjustment is similar to bankruptcy in that it is administered by the federal courts, but it differs in that the debtor is
allowed to continue to own most of his assets while paying
his creditors what the law specifies he must pay them from his
income. In many instances, a person who files for bankruptcy
would be better off had he sought debt adjustment under federal law.

Both bankruptcy and debt adjustment are administered by
federal courts. You may hear of bankruptcy procedures referred to as "Chapter 7," business reorganizations as "Chapter
11," and debt adjustment as "Chapter 13." These references are
to the Federal Bankruptcy Reform Act of 1978. Some state law
may apply through property exemptions—that is, property
that the bankrupt person does not have to relinquish to a
trustee for sale in order to pay creditors.

For someone with a steady income and assets that are not

exempt from the bankruptcy trustee, a debt adjustment may be in order. Declaring bankruptcy may be too drastic a step; the debtor may have gotten into some temporary financial trouble which can be resolved in time and with careful planning. On the other hand, if the debtor is at the end of his means and with little prospect of salvaging his finances, it may be that only a total discharge of his debts through bankruptcy can relieve him.

Debt adjustment must be formally approved. Under debt adjustment, the debtor proposes to the bankruptcy court a schedule of payments that will satisfy his current creditors within a specified period (usually three to five years). During this time, creditors must stop trying to collect their debts. The forms for filing for debt adjustment are available from the clerk of the local bankruptcy court (usually at the federal district courthouse), or from an office supply store.

Before filing for debt adjustment, you must fulfill several requirements. First, you must have a steady source of income. (At one time, debt adjustment was available only to wage earners, but now any steady source of income will suffice.) Second, you are limited to no more than $100,000 in unsecured debt (no collateral) and $350,000 in secured debt (secured by collateral). Third, your plan for payment must be submitted to the court in good faith, and the fees must be paid.

The costs of administering the plan will also be made a part of your payments. Each check you send to the trustee will include his payment as well as the fee of your lawyer (if you have one)—so you don't have to pay the bulk of this money before any proceedings start.

You do not need a lawyer to file a Chapter 13 proceeding. You can propose a plan to the court and represent yourself before creditors, in court. You may want to consult with an attorney to find out if Chapter 13 is the proper procedure for you, or you may want a lawyer to file the petitions and argue your case. You should base this decision solely on your confidence in your own capabilities. (Note that your attorney also becomes a creditor under the plan, and through it will get his fee over time.)

Bankruptcy also involves going to court. Bankruptcy is the total discharge of your debts (subject to a few exceptions, like student loans). Even taxes still owed are generally discharged. You are thus enabled to more or less completely satisfy your debts by giving your creditors, through the trustee, all of your assets not protected under federal or state law. Exempt assets include a certain amount for your house, a $1,200 exemption for a family car, unlimited household property valued under $200 per item, $750 in the tools of your trade, and certain insurance policies, pensions, and public benefits. (State laws also exempt certain property from bankruptcy seizure, so check with the bankruptcy clerk in your state's federal bankruptcy court for information about state exemptions.) Although the exemptions fall into certain categories, in some cases you can shift and carry over amounts from one category to another.

You may declare bankruptcy without the assistance of an attorney. But keep in mind that if the attorney charges $500 for filing the papers, and saves you $700 in property that you would not have claimed as exempt, he will have been very cost-effective.

You can file for bankruptcy only if you have not received a similar discharge from your debts within the past six years. Once the petition has been approved by the court, creditors must stop trying to collect their debts or harassing you. Also, bankruptcy discharges are only for debts created prior to your filing, not for those incurred afterwards. Likewise, a court will not grant a discharge from debts that it considers that you incurred in contemplation of bankruptcy—thus, you cannot go on a shopping spree, thinking that any debts can be erased through an impending bankruptcy.

Nor are you permitted to give your property away prior to bankruptcy, or give it to another person to hold for you to hide from the trustee and from creditors. You may, however, sell your nonexempt property and buy exempt property so that you can keep as much as possible through your bankruptcy.

Bankruptcy is a last resort. Declaring bankruptcy is a final and drastic step that should be contemplated only in the most dire circumstances. Under bankruptcy, you are asking the courts to protect you from creditors. Your debts would have to exceed your assets (possessions). Bankruptcy would either restructure your debts (protecting you temporarily, until you are able to pay them), or simply strike out all of your current debts (with a few exceptions like, for example, those incurred through fraud). But bankruptcy also makes it virtually impossible to obtain credit when you think you are able and ready to assume further credit obligations.

Bankruptcy is a function of the federal courts, and more information can be obtained from the clerk of the bankruptcy court in your state, or through an attorney who can further explain your rights and responsibilities (and the costs) of filing for bankruptcy.

A number of forms are needed to file for bankruptcy. They are available through the federal bankruptcy court or an office supply shop. The forms enable you to efficiently state your financial affairs (your wages, tax payments, refunds due, bank accounts, safe-deposit boxes, property in your hands and held by anyone else, and transfers of property that you have made within the last year). You will also list creditors, the amounts and circumstances of the debts, whether they are secured or unsecured by property or other collateral, and if any liens on your property have been made. You will note all personal and real property, as well as what you are claiming as exempt.

You will then meet with the creditors and trustees to make final the nature of your transfers to the trustee, and to determine what property you will be allowed to keep. For all of these steps, directions can be obtained from the bankruptcy-court clerk or from the trustee.

Your Family

6

Marriage and Divorce

Litigious terms, fat contentions, and flowing fees. —Milton, TRACTATE ON EDUCATION

FOR better or worse, the romance of marriage nowadays has increasingly given way to the drafting of premarital agreements concerning the rights of spouses and divisions of property. Likewise, the stigma once attached to divorce has been dissipated by the epidemic number of couples who split up.

There is nothing magical about a contract which specifies the rights and obligations of two people who are about to marry; it need not even be entirely formal. Similarly, your ability to handle your own divorce depends primarily on the complexity of your situation. By all means, you should first attempt reconciliation. But if your differences are irreconcilable—and if you and your spouse can agree on how the property should be divided (and if there are children receiving support, visitation, etc.)—then you should seriously consider representing yourselves.

Agreements between Spouses

Contracts between spouses can be written at any time. Contracts between husband and wife follow the same rules as do other contracts (see Chapter 1). The most common types of contracts between married persons are the antenuptial agreement (often an understanding about property, signed before the marriage ceremony) and the separation agreement (signed in contemplation of separation or divorce). A similar kind of contract is the cohabitation agreement, drawn up by people sharing a marital type of relationship but disdaining the traditional bonds of marriage itself.

Antenuptial, separation, and cohabitation agreements are attempts by people to specify their expectations of and promises to each other. They are also the means by which a couple can make their preferences known in writing (and possibly vary certain legal consequences) regarding support, division of property, or rights of inheritance—which the law would otherwise impose if no such contractual understanding existed. Courts will generally uphold these agreements (especially if they are in writing and signed by both parties).

The larger the assets, the greater the need for an attorney. Whenever there is a sizable amount of property involved, it is wise to obtain the advice of an attorney. Good legal advice could save tax dollars and prevent headaches later. Likewise, in any case where the parties' interests are competing or adversarial, separate legal counsel is necessary—that is, each person should have an attorney whenever one is waiving more valuable rights than the other, or when one person is financially dependent upon the other. This may seem extravagant, but the fact is that these agreements are worthless unless a court is willing to enforce them—and separate attorneys and full financial disclosure are the most convincing evidence to a judge that the contractual provisions are really fair and should be honored by both parties.

Under certain circumstances, a court can refuse to enforce a written, signed cohabitation, antenuptial, or separation agreement. A court may refuse to enforce a cohabitation agreement if it finds that sexual services were any part of the consideration, or if the judge feels that honoring cohabitation contracts encourages illicit relationships and would thus offend public policy. A separation agreement will not be honored if a court fails to find a valid marriage in existence at the time the agreement was signed. Neither an antenuptial nor a separation agreement will be enforced if a court finds that one of the parties did not fully disclose his or her assets at the time the agreement was made, that the provisions are simply unfair, that one party signed the agreement because of fraud, duress, or undue influence, or if the court decides that enforcement of the contract would be against public policy. Courts often refuse to enforce provisions in which a wife waived her rights to support or alimony, if the wife has no other means of supporting herself. (The courts in such cases hold that spouses have no right to relieve themselves of the duty of supporting each other where refusal to do so means one spouse must become a public charge by receiving welfare and the like.) Courts may also refuse to enforce an earlier separation agreement if the parties have since reconciled and later separated again.

All cohabitation and antenuptial (premarital) agreements should be custom-made. Cohabitation agreements must be tailored to fit the couple involved. The contract could vary significantly depending upon whether the couple view cohabitation as a temporary experiment, a trial marriage, or a chosen life style. In particular, the financial provisions should differ according to whether a short-term adventure or a lifetime commitment is envisioned.

The most important provisions are those that reflect the couple's understanding about common expenses and household chores, and the division of property and money if and when the parties do "divorce." If one person is agreeing to perform household domestic services in exchange for support, the agreement should specify the duration of the support obligation and the rights and duties (if any) of the parties after their living-together relationship terminates. The couple should also con-

sider if they want to include some degree of notice before one
of them can unilaterally terminate the relationship.

Modern antenuptial contracts (agreements made prior to an
impending marriage) include the couple's agreement regarding the wife's choice of surname. Many couples also include
provisions regarding the division of household responsibilities
and expenses, and their agreed-upon methods of making decisions about careers and changes of domicile. Most courts try to
honor such provisions, although they may not be legally enforceable. In a second-marriage situation, where the couple
wishes their individual estates to pass upon their death to the
children of their first marriages, the antenuptial contract
should include waivers of rights to the share of the other's
estate that is guaranteed by statute. Finally, the contract might
contain the couple's understanding regarding the ownership of
property and possessions acquired after marriage through the
efforts of only one party. A couple living in a community-
property state might prefer to keep their holdings as in common law, while couples in a common-law state might consider
the community-property system more to their liking.

There is a difference between the community-property and
common-law methods of regarding property acquired during
marriage. In the *community-property* states (Arizona, California, Idaho, Louisiana, Nevada, New Mexico, Texas, and
Washington), all property acquired by either spouse during
marriage is held as community property. This means that upon
divorce, the property is divided equally. Similarly, at the death
of one spouse, half of the community property goes to the heirs
of the deceased, and the other half to the surviving spouse.

In *common-law* states, the person who buys and holds legal
title to a piece of property owns it. Therefore, a husband who
buys stocks, bonds, houses, cars, and other property in his own
name owns these items free of any claim by his wife upon
divorce—unless the state's divorce statute allows a judge to
order an *equitable distribution*. In common-law states with
equitable-distribution provisions, the judge decides what will

be most fair to the parties, without reference to who owns legal title. A judge with powers to equitably distribute marital property generally has more discretion than a judge in a community-property state; the latter must divide the marital property in half regardless of the fact that one party may have a far higher earning potential than the other.

A separation agreement should be particular. The separation agreement should specify the division of property which the couple have agreed to, or state that the couple have already split the property between the two of them in a manner satisfactory to both. The contract should spell out the amount of support or alimony to be paid by one spouse to the other, *or* contain a clause indicating that both parties waive the right to any support from the other. If there are children, the contract should specify who has custody, what rights of visitation are allowed to the noncustodial parent, and the amount of child support that the noncustodial parent has agreed to contribute. Separation agreements generally contain a provision waiving any rights to claim against the other's estate. If the couple expect to petition under a no-fault ground of divorce, the contract should contain the clause that irreconcilable differences have arisen between the parties, and that they are now living, or intend immediately to live, separate and apart.

Divorce and Separation

No-fault divorce is increasingly common. In every state there are specific grounds for divorce. In all but Illinois and South Dakota, there is at least one ground for divorce in which neither fault nor blame is placed on one of the parties for ostensibly "causing" the divorce. These no-fault grounds are most appropriate in situations where both partners agree to end the marriage, and recognize that placing blame or fault serves no useful purpose. There are a number of no-fault grounds for divorce (or "dissolution"—the euphemism for divorce used in some no-fault states), including irreconcilable differences, irretrievable breakdown of the relationship, incompatibility, or simply mutual voluntary separation for a specific period of time. There are numerous other grounds for divorce. They vary from state to state. Residency requirements range from six weeks to one year, although they are usually from ninety days to six months. For a complete list of grounds for divorce by state, see Appendix I.

Divorcing couples do not necessarily need lawyers. In states that provide a no-fault ground for divorce, a couple not wishing to contest the dissolution of their marriage, without children, and without much property to split, could easily file their own papers. An uncontested divorce is one where both parties want out, and agree on the grounds for divorce, a division of property, support, child custody, and visitation rights. Note, however, that a genuinely uncontested divorce before the intervention of attorneys is rare except in cases where the marriage was short, the marital property is minimal, and both parties are self-supporting (i.e., no alimony is necessary). Unless one of the parties is extraordinarily generous, the general rule is that the spouse who is going to need alimony should get an attorney to make sure his or her financially vulnerable position is not exploited.

In a genuinely uncontested divorce, the couple should sit down and draft a separation agreement outlining the details of property distribution, spousal and child support, visitation rights, etc. Then one party should call the clerk of the court that handles divorces in their county or city, and ask to see an example of a properly drafted no-fault divorce petition. Many clerks are helpful, especially if you make it clear that you are just asking for a model and not a petition perfectly suited to your situation (which would involve legal advice).

File a properly drafted petition for a divorce decree. Ask the court clerk for a sample form.

After you file a properly drafted petition for a divorce decree with the clerk for the divorce court in your domicile (your legal residence), you must arrange for *service of process* upon your spouse—notice of the proceedings, so that the court is assured the other party has been fully informed and can participate if it is felt necessary. The court clerk can tell you the different ways by which adequate notice can be rendered. If your spouse has any objections to the proceedings, he or she must indicate to the court the need for a full-scale hearing. If an adversarial hearing is scheduled, hire yourself an attorney.

If your spouse ignores the notice or indicates consent to the divorce, after some period of time (each state varies) the court will probably notify you of a hearing date. This court appearance is not necessary in all states. Where it is, it generally consists of the court asking you a few questions about the same matters you covered in your petition. You may also need a witness to corroborate your residence in the state or the basis for divorce (for example, that the parties are in fact living apart). Finally, the court will issue a divorce decree—which may have an effective date many months after your court appearance, depending upon the practice in your state. You should not remarry until you have the divorce decree in your hands and it is actually in effect. Marriage to anyone else before the divorce decree is effective makes you guilty of bigamy. Be careful to avoid a "fault ground for divorce" (such as adultery) during the waiting period.

If you think there is a possibility of reaching agreement with your spouse, consider mediation. In many cases, husbands and wives agree that they are going to get divorced but aren't able to work out the financial matters or arrange for custody and visitation rights regarding the children. Increasingly, couples are turning away from lawyers and toward mediators as a means of resolving these kinds of controversies. Why? Because litigation is inevitably divisive and has particularly harmful effects on the children. In addition, mediation can produce innovative solutions that are impossible in a courtroom.

Mediation in divorce is a relatively new development. Briefly stated, a trained mediator (who may happen to be a lawyer but usually is not) meets with the parties, tries to identify their needs, and helps them to find a solution that best suits all of their interests. He or she doesn't take sides or arbitrate, but tries to let the parties reach their own accommodation.

In many cases, the mediator will insist, or at least strongly urge, the parties to have their own lawyers look over their agreement—but only *after* the basic terms have been worked out and reduced to writing. This kind of "safety valve" is generally money well spent, since lawyers can often spot places where the agreement is unclear or where there may be tax advantages to both parties in constructing the deal a little differently. Some couples also use lawyers as back-room advisers during the process, but not as active participants.

The use of lawyers as backup support, rather than as principal negotiators and advocates, offers another benefit beyond reducing rancor: the attorneys' fees will eat up a far smaller share of whatever size pie the couple has to divide between them.

There are other ways to part. One can also end a marriage by obtaining an annulment (under appropriate circumstances), or sue for "separate maintenance."

An *annulment* is a judicial decision that a marriage never really took place. This could be because one of the parties entered into the marriage through fraud or duress; because a state law forbidding marriage between minors or certain close relatives was violated; because one of the parties was insane, drunk, or under the influence of drugs so that he or she did not know the nature, meaning, or consequences of the marriage contract; or because one of the parties was still married to someone else.

Generally, if a marriage is annulled rather than terminated by divorce, neither spouse is entitled to alimony or separate maintenance. There are exceptions to this rule; check your state's laws.

If a married couple choose no longer to live together as husband and wife, yet for religious or personal reasons they do not want a legal divorce, they can enter into a contractual agreement for separate maintenance. This is often called a legal separation by laymen. This kind of separation agreement spells out the rights and duties of the spouses to each other, their property, and their children. Although under the terms of such an agreement each party may live apart, free from harassment or control of the other, the couple are still legally married. In general, the separate-maintenance arrangement is merely an interim step on the way to eventual divorce. It is primarily used on a permanent basis in cases where both spouses firmly disapprove of divorce but can accept a separate-maintenance arrangement.

Alimony

Alimony is not hard to understand. Alimony is an amount a court may order one spouse to pay the other in financial support—either while the divorce action is pending (called temporary alimony or *pendente lite*), or after the divorce has been granted (called permanent alimony, although it may last for only a limited number of years). If the couple are unable to agree upon a figure between themselves, the trial judge will decide the amount.

If a voluntary agreement cannot be made as to the amount of alimony, lawyers are usually necessary in order to present the parties' best possible cases to the court.

The husband does not always pay the wife alimony. As a result of equal-rights amendments passed in various states and a recent Supreme Court decision, the party better able to afford alimony may have to pay. In addition, he or she may have to pay the spouse's attorney as well as his or her own, if the court so orders.

You can sue for nonpayment of alimony. If the spousal support was part of a purely out-of-court separation agreement, you can sue for breach of contract in a small-claims court. If the amount in arrears is within the small-claims court's limit, you can claim it yourself without an attorney.

But if the support was court-ordered alimony, or if a separation agreement was incorporated in the court order, only that court can discipline the recalcitrant party. Hire a lawyer, and ask the court to award attorney's fees as well. The court will order the nonpaying party to appear to explain why the payments were not made. Unless he or she can prove convincing extenuating circumstances, the nonpaying party may be jailed for contempt of court until he or she complies with the alimony-payment order.

Custody

Get a lawyer unless you can agree. Unless the other parent is agreeable to your having custody, the best advice is to hire the best divorce lawyer you can afford and prepare for a battle. The custody decision will be made by a judge on the basis of what is thought to be in the best interest (physically and emotionally) of the child—regardless of any agreement by the parties.

Visiting rights are usually granted. The noncustodial parent has a right to reasonable visitation rights, unless the custodial parent can prove to the court that such visitation rights would be dangerous to the child's physical or mental health. What is reasonable depends upon the individual circumstances—such as the parents' work schedules, the distance between the parents' homes, and the child's own school schedule.

The best arrangements for visitation rights are those worked out by the parties themselves. But where the parties absolutely can't agree, a judge will decide custody matters, and those who refuse to follow the court order can be jailed for contempt of court.

There can be voluntary agreements regarding child support. Child support is the amount of money paid by a noncustodial parent to help pay for the support of the children raised by the parent with custody. Unlike alimony, child support is generally a joint obligation of the parents. Most courts will consent to any agreement made between the parents regarding child support, so long as the judge is satisfied that the provisions are in the best interest of the child.

Since payments for child support are not taxable to the recipient but alimony *is*, make sure that your agreement clearly separates the two amounts; otherwise, the lump sum will be considered like alimony and taxed. Note that child support is tax-deductible by the one who pays it, while alimony is not; hence, it is usually mutually advantageous for divorcing couples with children to arrange for child support rather than alimony, especially if the children are young. You should also specify what effect remarriage or a child's age will have on the agreement.

Note that the right to child support—unlike alimony—cannot be waived. Parents have the duty to support their children. Thus, even if the custodial parent had previously made the mistake of knowingly and voluntarily waiving the right to child support in a signed, written agreement, a court can still impose child-support duties upon a noncustodial parent, where the court believes it is necessary for the child.

The custodial parent cannot deny visitation rights when an ex-spouse falls behind in alimony or child-support payments. Child support and child-visitation rights are independent. That one party is breaching his or her part of the agreement (either the duty to provide child support or the duty to allow reasonable visitation) does *not* excuse the other from living up to his or her part of the agreement. It is conceivable that *both* parties could be held in contempt of court and either fined or even jailed until they comply with the court order.

Residency is important. Keep in mind that, if the other spouse is not a resident of your state, you can't get alimony or child support in your state unless he or she consents to jurisdiction. The alternative is to sue where the other spouse lives, but that is likely to be expensive and inconvenient.

7

Adoption and Guardianship

Guard us, guide us, keep us, feed us,
For we have no help but Thee.
    —James Edmeston, SACRED LYRICS

ADOPTION is the act of taking someone else's child into your own family, as if it had been born to you, and giving it all the rights and duties of a blood relative. A legal adoption is the procedure which establishes that relationship, and terminates the rights and duties of the natural birth-parents. In short, an adoption decree creates real parents by law.

A guardian is a person legally given the power and duty to take care of someone who by age or disability is considered incapable of administering his or her own affairs. Parents (whether by birth or adoption) are considered the natural guardians of minors, but guardians are not considered the parents of the person entrusted to their care. It is a trust rather than a parental relationship, and regulated by entirely different state laws from those which regulate adoption.

In either case, a lawyer is generally not necessary.

There is a difference between a stepparent adoption and an agency adoption. A stepparent adoption takes place when someone adopts a spouse's child from a prior marriage. In an

71

agency adoption, the birth-parents *surrender* (give up all rights to) the child to an appropriate agency, which then places it for adoption with suitable adoptive parents.

You must be an adult to adopt. State laws vary, but the general rule is that any person over the age of twenty-one can adopt. Many states require that the adopting parent be at least ten or fifteen years older than the child, although such a provision is generally not applied in cases of stepparent adoption. Legally, you don't have to be married to adopt a child. Realistically, it is more difficult for an unmarried person to convince both an adoption agency and the court that adoption by a single parent is in the child's best interest. If you are married, all states require that the adoption petition be made jointly, or at least be consented to by the other spouse (usually the case in a stepparent adoption).

Adults themselves can sometimes be adopted. All state laws provide for the adoption of minors—ordinarily defined as a child under twenty-one years of age. Adult adoption (generally done for reasons involving inheritance) is permissible in most but not all states. Where adult adoption is allowed, it is generally a simple procedure, since the stringent provisions designed to protect vulnerable minors are often eliminated.

Do-it-yourself adoptions are feasible. In a stepparent situation where both birth-parents consent (that is, the spouse/birth-parent and the other birth-parent), adoption can generally be accomplished by the drafting and filing of a few papers. In such cases a nonlawyer could easily arrange an adoption by himself. If an agency adoption is involved, or if there is any difficulty obtaining consent from both birth-parents, you'd better hire an attorney. Adoption under those circumstances is often complicated and emotionally charged, and the expertise of a knowledgeable lawyer is important.

Similarly, any birth-parent who has surrendered a child to an agency or otherwise consented to an adoption—and now has a change of heart—should immediately consult an attorney knowledgeable in such matters. Timing is of the essence, because once a final adoption decree is issued by the court, it will probably be too late to regain custody.

There are various formalities involved in legally adopting a child. Once the prospective parents have in mind the child to adopt, the legal process consists of these steps:

1. Obtaining the necessary consents
2. Filing an adoption petition in court
3. Giving appropriate notice to interested parties
4. Having an investigation done (if required by the court)
5. Participating in a hearing

When these steps have been completed, the court can issue an adoption decree.

Consent is a prerequisite. Although state laws vary, both children and natural parents must generally consent before an adoption will be approved by a court.

The child's consent must be obtained if he or she is old enough to give it. Some states say a ten-year-old is capable of consent, but the most frequent age used in statutes is fourteen years. As a practical matter, you should always try to gain the consent of any child who is old enough to know what is going on—since nothing is lost even if such consent is not legally necessary. The consent can be a simple statement, witnessed and dated.

Both natural birth-parents must approve unless they have previously surrendered the child to an agency, or their parental rights were terminated in a prior court proceeding. If the whereabouts of one of the birth-parents is unknown and efforts to locate him have been unsuccessful, the adoption may be granted as if he had consented.

If both natural birth-parents are dead, the consent of a guardian, next of kin, or state-authorized agency must be given before an adoption will be approved by a court.

The natural birth-parents don't always have to consent before
their child can be adopted by strangers. If birth-parents surrender a child to an authorized agency, their parental rights
are considered *voluntarily* terminated. The child may be
adopted by others without the birth-parents' consents (or even
knowledge), so long as the agency itself approves of the adoption.

Likewise, if it is determined in a prior legal proceeding that
the birth-parents have persistently neglected or abandoned
their child, or are unfit for some other serious reason, their
parental rights are *involuntarily* terminated. In such cases the
birth-parents have no right to consent—or to refuse to consent
—to their child's adoption by others.

Consent forms need not be complicated. An adequate consent
(combined with a waiver of notice, where the parties are willing) can be as simple as a signed statement to this effect:

> I, John Doe, hereby consent to the adoption of my minor
> daughter, Mary Doe, by Henry Smith, and to the changing of
> Mary Doe's name to Mary Smith. I hereby voluntarily join in
> adoption petition and waive any requirement that I be given
> further notice of these proceedings.

If the consent has to be "verified," add another sentence:

> I do solemnly swear and affirm under the penalties of perjury
> that the contents of the foregoing document are true and cor-
> rect and that my consent is given of my own free will and voli-
> tion without any promises or coercion whatsoever.

Sign and date the document in front of a notary public, unless
the court clerk has absolutely assured you that notarization is
unnecessary.

An adoption petition is a formal document. It is filed by the
adopting parents in the proper court, setting forth information
about the child and its natural and adopting parents. Generally, it reflects the consents that have been obtained (attaching

copies is advisable), announces which if any of the necessary parties have waived further notice, and requests the court to approve the adoption and, if appropriate, to change the child's name.

State statutes are usually specific in indicating what information must be included in an adoption petition. Usually required are the name, sex, residence, age, race, and religion of all parties; the date and place of birth of the child; any property the child owns; the marital status of the birth-parents and the adoptive parents; the length of time the child has resided with the adoptive parents; how the child came into their home; and, if the child is in the custody of an agency, a statement of how such custody was acquired. In many states, if the birth-mother is unmarried, information regarding the birth-father is not required.

If you are a stepparent wishing to draft and file an adoption petition (where consent is not a problem), you should call the clerk of the court that handles adoptions. He can instruct you how to buy the appropriate form or can show you a properly drafted adoption petition. Once you have a model to use, adapting it to your own situation should be easy. The clerk will also know how much it costs, whether the consents and waivers of notice should be notarized, verified (see page 74), or witnessed, as well as other technicalities that might be required.

Proper legal notice is a very important and often highly technical requirement. Generally, the same parties who must consent to the adoption are legally entitled to notice (i.e., to be told when and where the court proceedings will take place)— unless a waiver of notice was included in the consent form. But each jurisdiction has different rules. The court clerk can inform you who is to get and how you are to give proper notice.

The court does not always order an investigation. In cases of an uncontested stepparent adoption, the court may decide that an investigation is unnecessary. In other cases, the judge will usually ask the appropriate agency to provide detailed information regarding the adoptive parents and the circumstances surrounding the adoption, in order to make certain that adoption by the petitioning parties is in the best interest of the child.

The hearing is often informal. A court hearing may be waived in the stepparent adoption situation where all the parties have been notified and have consented to the adoption. Otherwise, after proper notice has been given and an investigation made by the appropriate state agency, a judicial hearing will be held. It often is informal, held in the judge's chambers. The prospective adoptive parents must be present as well as the child if it is old enough to give consent. The judge will examine the interested parties and consider the investigative report. Although the court is not bound to accept the recommendation of the report, it carries great weight and is seldom ignored. The court may also hear witnesses and generally ask questions to satisfy itself as to the advisability of the adoption. In all states, the court's primary concern is for the welfare and best interests of the child.

Decrees are not always final. After the hearing, if the court approves the adoption, it will issue either an interlocutory (temporary) or a final decree. With an interlocutory decree, the court has issued conditional approval of the adoption, and will reconsider the application at a later date (generally six months to a year in the future). During this intervening period, the child lives in the home of the prospective adopters. Usually there is some sort of appropriate agency supervision— often involving visits to the home to see how the child is getting along. Interlocutory decrees may be revoked at any time during the trial period, either by the judge on his own or at the request of the birth-parents, the adopting parents, or the supervising agency. If all goes well during this trial period, however, the court will issue a final decree approving the adoption with or without another hearing. Many states do not explicitly provide for an interlocutory decree, but achieve a similar effect by requiring that the child must have lived in the adoptive parents' home for a specified period of time before a final decree will be approved. This requirement will often be waived by the court where there is good reason to do so, such as the stepparent adoption situation.

Birth-parents can sometimes regain custody. Some states allow a birth-parent the absolute right to regain custody—unless the parental rights have been involuntarily terminated in a prior legal proceeding—before a final decree has been issued. Some states never allow a surrender to be rescinded unless there was evidence of fraud or duress which made the surrender involuntary. In the majority of states, however, a parent may regain custody within a fixed period of time (usually ranging from six months to one year after the surrender)—during which no final adoption decree can be issued.

Once a final adoption decree has been issued by a court, it is virtually impossible for a birth-parent to regain custody.

The law makes it difficult for an adoptee to learn the identity of his or her natural birth-parents. While it is never illegal for an adoptee to try to learn the identity of his or her birth-parents, the law in most states hinders rather than assists the adoptee's search. As of 1982 the only two states that did not automatically seal all adoption records were Alabama and South Dakota. In the rest of the states, sealed-record statutes prohibit the inspection of records which would disclose the identity of the adoptee's birth-parents, except upon a showing to a court of good cause. In Connecticut, Iowa, Michigan, Nebraska, North Dakota, and Virginia, the court can open the otherwise sealed adoption record if the birth-parent is contacted and gives consent. In Florida, Maine, Michigan, Minnesota, Nevada, and New Jersey, the states have created registries which will unite adoptees with their birth-parents if they both indicate their interest in reunion.

An adult adoptee (or a birth-parent) interested in searching should contact a search group such as Adoptees' Liberation Movement (ALMA), which is based in New York but has branches in almost every state. People in these groups are far more knowledgeable about how to conduct a search than the average attorney. ALMA also maintains a nationwide registry—the largest of its kind.

Adoption agencies generally encourage birth-parents to provide updated information (especially medical information) which will be given to any adoptee who requests it. In addition, most agencies will release nonidentifying information —genetic and medical data, and sometimes a description of the circumstances which led the birth-parents to surrender the child for adoption—to adoptees who request it.

Guardianships

Guardians are usually appointed out of necessity. Since the parents are considered the joint natural guardians of their minor children, there is generally no need to provide a child with a guardian unless both parents are dead. But it is wise to appoint a guardian for minor children in your will, in case your spouse predeceases you or you both die in a common accident. Guardians are also appointed for persons who are mentally incapable of handling their own affairs.

No special terminology is required. Simply be sure that the proposed guardian is clearly identified, and his or her authority is clearly expressed (i.e., whether the guardian is given custody over the child's person, property, or both). It is also wise to provide an alternate or co-guardian. Since most states require those acting in a trust capacity to post bond (to insure honest performance), it would be a convenience and consideration to your chosen guardian if you explicitly waive (give up) any bond requirement otherwise demanded by your state. It is also wise to include instructions regarding care, maintenance, and education of the child, and the conditions under which the guardian should consider his duties to the child terminated (such as when the child reaches age eighteen).

Some states (e.g., Maryland) do not consider will-appointed guardians binding, but courts generally honor such appointments.

Guardianship is heavily regulated. State statutes are designed to protect the rights and interests of handicapped, disabled, or otherwise incompetent persons from those who would try to take advantage of their vulnerability. Except by way of a last will and testament, being appointed a guardian is a complicated process involving consents, physicians' approvals, and proper notice prior to a judicial hearing where the judge decides whether to approve the petition for guardianship. Such appointments are probably best handled with the assistance of a competent attorney.

Where adult children would like to take care of their elderly parents, a far easier solution is to obtain a power of attorney while the parent is still of sound mind. No court approval is necessary prior to acting under a power of attorney given by someone who is considered mentally capable.

But remember, a power of attorney can always be revoked by its author—even if he or she is no longer of sound mind.

8

Powers of Attorney

What is the price of your voice?
—Juvenal, SATIRES

ANYONE who wants to have his or her affairs administered by
someone else (as, for example, where geographical distance is
a problem) can do so by means of a document called a power
of attorney.

A *power of attorney* is simply a written legal paper in which
the principal (an individual, a partnership, or a corporation)
appoints an agent (an individual, a partnership, or a corporation), and gives that agent the authority and power to act in
his behalf. Authority can be general (extending over the
principal's person and all his or her property), or specific
(limited, for example, to the sale of a particular house or the
handling of a particular lawsuit). It can grant power to borrow
money, pay bills, collect debts, manage a business, or sell
property. Having the power of an attorney has nothing to do
with being a lawyer, although a lawyer may be given a power
of attorney.

Practically anyone can create a power-of-attorney relationship.
A power of attorney can be authorized by any person who is of
sound mind and who can communicate rational decisions con-

cerning his health or financial affairs. If a person is mentally or physically disabled to the extent that he or she cannot so communicate, it is too late to create a power-of-attorney relationship. At this point a lawyer should be consulted to determine whether legal-guardianship proceedings are necessary or advisable.

It's easy to draft a document creating a power of attorney. Historically, it has been the common practice to begin the document creating a power of attorney with the phrase "Know All Persons by These Presents"—but those words are not essential. The instrument should set out the principal's name and address, and those of the agent. It should indicate the date or specific event (such as illness or disability) upon which the power of attorney is to take effect. The document should expressly outline the specific powers given to the agent (that is, state for what purposes the agent is to act). Finally, it should explain what effect the disability or death of the principal should have, and the date or event, if any, upon which the agent's power of attorney is to be terminated. The principal should sign the document and deliver it to the agent (keeping, of course, a copy for his own records).

Examples of general and specific powers of attorney can be found in Appendix II.

A power-of-attorney document should be notarized. It is in the agent's interest to have the document creating a power of attorney notarized, even though that is not legally necessary for the authorization to be valid and binding. Notarization may be of some protection against later claims that the agent exerted undue influence over the principal, or that the principal was not of sound mind at the time the power was created.

In addition, if the powers granted concern the conveyance of real estate by the agent on behalf of the principal, the formalities associated with the making of a valid deed may apply. That is, the power of attorney may have to be witnessed, acknowledged, and recorded. If you are in doubt, call the clerk of the land-records office where the property is located, and ask what measures should be taken.

A power of attorney is not permanent. In some states, a power of attorney automatically terminates when the principal becomes disabled or dies (unless the principal has given instructions to the contrary in the instrument). A well-drawn document creating a power of attorney should include the date or event, if any, upon which the power is to be terminated. Notwithstanding such a provision, however, it is always best to formally end a power-of-attorney relationship by means of another signed written document, again delivered to the agent himself. If there is any concern that the agent might continue to hold himself out to others as if he were still acting on your behalf, it is a wise precaution to send notice of the termination of the relationship to all those who might be affected.

9

Changing Names

I cannot tell what the dickens his name is.
—Shakespeare
THE MERRY WIVES OF WINDSOR

It has always been the common law that a person may change his or her own name without resorting to legal proceedings—if there is no intention to defraud, if no one else is adversely affected, and if it would not be against public policy. (Courts have refused to change a man's name to a number, and a feminist's name from Zimmerman to Zimmerwoman.) If you use the new name consistently and exclusively, your name change is accomplished by such usage and habit. The name assumed is your legal name for all purposes, just as though you had carried it from birth or it had been provided by court order.

A change of name may also be accomplished via a court order or decree—although this method is no more legal than the common-law method explained above. It does have the practical advantage, however, of providing an official record, and is often demanded by governmental agencies before they will issue a new Social Security card or driver's license, or change names on a deed or voter's card.

A woman's surname does not always automatically and legally change to that of her husband after marriage. If the woman adopts the custom of taking her husband's surname, and uses his surname as her own consistently and exclusively, the change of name is accomplished by the common-law method of usage and habit. This practice is so established that governmental agencies generally honor a woman's request for their records to reflect her name change without demanding a court order. However, if the woman consistently and exclusively uses her maiden name after marriage, the recent legal trend is to accept the rather obvious conclusion that the wife's name was not changed by the simple fact of her marriage.

Court orders can change names. There are three kinds of court orders that can involve changes of name: adoption decrees, divorce decrees, and change-of-name decrees. Since the first two orders are discussed elsewhere in this book, only the third will be explained here.

You do not generally need an attorney to obtain a court order changing your name unless there is an adversarial proceeding. Under normal situations, you should be able to buy a copy of a petition-to-change-a-name form. Ask the clerk of the court that handles change-of-name proceedings. Aside from the petition, the change-of-name procedure is so simple that a layman should easily be able to handle it.

Although state requirements vary, in general there are three parts to the process of changing your name by a court order: the petition; publication or notice; and the court decree.

Different information is contained in the court petition. Every state has a statute prescribing the procedure by which a person may change his name, as well as the specific information that must be contained in the petition addressed to the court. Generally, the petition must be in writing and signed by the person seeking the name change. In most states, it must specify the former name, the date and place of birth, and the reasons for the name change; the current age and address; and the proposed new name. In some states, you must say whether you have ever been convicted of a crime or declared a bankrupt, and whether there are any judgments or liens or court proceedings pending under the old name. It is wise to include a statement to the effect that this change of name is not for fraudulent purposes or to avoid creditors.

When you call the clerk of the court to ask about buying or seeing a petition to use as a model, also ask whether the petition has to be verified and/or notarized. *Verification* is done by adding a statement to the effect that the petitioner swears that the facts contained in the petition are true, and if necessary the petitioner is prepared to testify to them under oath or prove them through documents.

Publication is required. Publication is the act of giving some type of notice to the general public of the petitioner's intention to change his name. Anyone who objects to the name change (for example, a creditor or a person with the same name) then has the opportunity to make such objections known to the court, which will try to balance the competing interests.

Publication is generally accomplished by placing a notice in a local newspaper. The clerk of the court will be able to give more specific details about the procedure followed in your jurisdiction. It might also be useful to ask the clerk under what circumstances publication by newspaper can be waived (dispensed with) and some other less expensive method used in its stead. In many states, newspaper publication can be waived if the name change involves a minor and both parents consent to the new name, or if the name change is requested by an adult who has been known by the "new" name all of his life and whose "old" name was never used except on his birth certificate.

The court decree makes it official. If sufficient time has elapsed after publication of the notice of the petitioner's intention to change his name, and no one has objected (certainly the usual case), the judge will issue a decree stating that the name requested is now the petitioner's legal name for all purposes. Once you have the court decree, you can get your name changed on your driver's license and Social Security card simply by showing your decree.

10

Health Matters

Health care is a right, not a privilege.
                    —National Free Clinic Council

Dᴇᴛᴇʀᴍɪɴɪɴɢ whether you need a lawyer in a wide variety of
health matters is facilitated by knowledge of your basic legal
rights—concerning everything from access to medical records
to protesting a bill for fees or services. It's also important to be
assertive. The medical establishment can be extremely difficult
to penetrate.

Access to Records

Medical records are kept in a variety of places. Your medical
records are those kept by your private doctor, clinic, or hospital of visits, tests, forms that you may have signed, billings and
payments, and other personal information.

The Joint Committee on Accreditation of Hospitals, a voluntary organization to which most hospitals belong, has developed guidelines for what records must be kept on each patient.
They include any consent forms you have signed, your medical
history (supplied either by you or your doctors), records of
physical examinations, laboratory reports, doctors' orders, and
the record of your treatment and progress in that hospital. The

contents and the completeness of these records are also regulated by state laws.

Your medical records should be important to you. As a patient, you should be aware of your condition and the progress you have made in your treatments. This information should be useful in discussing your problems with your doctors and the hospital staff, and to allow you to make informed choices about treatment. You can also evaluate the quality of the care you have received—as well as protect your legal rights if any procedure has been done that you have not approved. A review of your medical records can also help you determine if you have been properly charged for the services rendered.

Once you decipher the horrendous handwriting for which doctors are notorious, medical records are not difficult to understand. You may need a medical dictionary or glossary of terms relating to your specific condition.

The paper on which your records actually appear is owned by the health-care provider (the hospital, doctor, or clinic). The X-ray pictures that the radiologist has taken are his property. But you have a right to know what information is contained in those documents, as well as the right to reasonably inspect and copy them if you wish.

It is not always easy to copy or inspect your records. Unfortunately, many states do not allow patients easy access to their medical records. Such jurisdictions may feel that you do not have any rights to your X-ray films because they were ancillary to your medical treatment: you did not commission a photographer, but rather asked a medical professional for an opinion about your condition; the physician took the pictures as an aid in making a diagnosis.

In these states, your medical records may be gotten only through a subpoena or court order. The hitch is that you must sue your doctor or hospital before the court can order them to produce your records. This situation prompts the filing of many needless malpractice suits against doctors and hospitals.

Many of these providers will relinquish your records, if requested, in order to avoid a lawsuit.

Other states allow access to your records if you ask for them in writing. You may be charged a reasonable fee for locating and copying them.

You can avoid the problem of access by having your doctor agree ahead of time that you will be entitled to keep your X-rays or other pertinent data or at least have access to them.

If the hospital is run by the federal government, or by a state with its own freedom-of-information law, you can get access to your records more easily. Ask to see the hospital's Freedom of Information Act Officer for details on how to initiate the process.

Confidentiality

Generally, your records are confidential. If they are doctor's records, only the doctor and his staff should have access. If they are hospital records, only hospital personnel who participate in your care have access—not nurses or other aides who happen to be on the floor.

Some types of records are open to certain officials or health agencies. For example, all treatment received for bullet or knife wounds, or injuries sustained in an automobile accident or under other violent circumstances, must be reported to the local police. Suspected child-abuse cases are referred to state or local social-service agencies. Records of some contagious diseases, birth defects, or drug abuse are sent to state or local health agencies.

If you tell someone something with the understanding that it will not be repeated, a confidential relationship has been created. Medical records and other information about your health are considered to be confidential records. Under the physicians' Hippocratic oath and the American Medical Association's Principles of Medical Ethics, a doctor is forbidden to disclose any fact that has come to his attention as a result of the doctor-patient relationship. A physician who violates your confidence can face professional disciplinary action, as well as a lawsuit brought by you. Hospitals and other health-care providers are under a similar legal duty.

Confidentiality applies to information about your spouse or other relative. You do not have an automatic right to medical information regarding your spouse or other relative, although they may grant permission to have you included in any discussion with the health-care provider, or grant you access to medical records.

An exception to this rule, of course, is parents' rights to information about their children. Parents are generally responsible for making decisions about the health of minor children—those under eighteen or twenty-one, depending on the state laws. However, some medical procedures can be contracted by minor children, and a confidential relationship is invoked which cannot be penetrated by the parents. Check your local laws, or call a health agency in your state or county, to determine what rules of confidentiality govern a given medical situation.

There is little difference between confidentiality and the courtroom's doctor-patient privilege. Basically, the doctor-patient privilege that may be invoked in court is the same as the confidentiality rule. The testimonial privilege belongs to the patient, not the doctor. If a doctor is asked in court to tell about the patient's condition, the doctor must refuse unless the patient has previously released him to testify. But the law in this area differs from state to state, and there are certain exceptions to the privilege, such as if the patient has put his condition or treatment in contention by a suit against the doctor, or if the legality of a document signed by the patient is in question. Again, this privilege differs from state to state; but it is always the right of the patient, and not of the doctor. The patient makes the decision as to whether the doctor can or cannot speak.

Informed consent is necessary before you are treated. The law requires that, except in certain emergency situations, you grant your consent before any medical procedures are performed on you. Not only must you consent, but you must do so willingly and understanding the possible consequences. If your doctor says that you need a certain operation, he must first tell you the risks involved, alternative therapy available, as well as the possible results of that operation (e.g., slow recovery, possible lameness, chronic illness or disability). Anything less will fall short of the required informed consent. A doctor operating without informed consent is liable to both professional discipline and a lawsuit (for battery or malpractice).

It is important that you be able to make a clear and intelligent choice. Do not be afraid to ask questions until you are satisfied with the answers. Read all consent forms provided by the doctor or hospital, before signing them. A conscientious doctor will not pressure you into an operation before you know the risks involved. Listen carefully; when necessary, take notes.

In almost all cases when the patient is of sound mind and conscious, informed consent procedures must be followed. But if the patient cannot consent to a procedure because of mental incompetence or some other disability, a court must appoint a guardian who, after having the procedure explained to him, can himself make an informed consent. If there is no time for such an appointment (such as in the case of emergency treatment), informed consent is implied—but must not be exceeded. For example, if a person is brought into an emergency room unconscious and needing stomach surgery, no further surgery (such as an appendectomy) can be undertaken.

There are other situations when the court may be asked to appoint a guardian. If a parent refuses to consent to a blood transfusion for a child because of religious or other beliefs—and the transfusion is necessary to save the child's life—the court will appoint a guardian who then has the power to consent to the transfusion. If an elderly person needs an operation and is not of the proper mind to make a clear and rational decision, the court can also appoint a guardian to make such a decision. The guardian may or may not have to be a relative. State laws vary on this subject.

You have the right to a second opinion. You have every right to ask your doctor to allow you to see another doctor before consenting to any form of treatment. A good doctor, who feels he has properly diagnosed your problem, should have no qualms about your seeing another physician to verify his opinion. Do not think that you are insulting the doctor by asking for time before giving your consent. Doctors should understand your concern: some even expect you to ask for a second opinion on major operations. Remember that you have a right to a second opinion; even if you do not exercise that right, be aware of it.

Some insurance plans *require* you to get a second opinion before they pay for health claims resulting from major medical treatments. Check with your insurer before committing yourself to a course of treatment.

There is a Patients' Bill of Rights. The American Hospital Association has developed a Hospital Patients' Bill of Rights. When you are admitted to a hospital, ask for a copy if you have not received it. Most hospitals are members of AHA, and are thus committed to guarantee you these basic rights while you are under their care: to accept or reject any visitors, to refuse medication if you so desire, not to be disrobed for any time longer than necessary and to have a staff person of your same sex present at any physical examination (a right that should also exist in the doctor's office), and to consent to physical examinations (and while in a teaching hospital, to refuse to be examined by medical students or groups of interns). These rights are augmented by some state laws.

Bills

Talk to your doctor if you have a question about the bill. As with any other dispute over fees or costs, you should first bring your complaint to the attention of the health-care provider who has billed you. Try to come to a reasonable agreement with the provider, and to effect a compromise between his claim and what you think you owe him. With hospital services, there are often charges by individuals with whom you have had no direct contact. Do not feel intimidated against asking for justification of specific items on your bill.

If you are being treated by a clinic, go to the administrative officer of the clinic. If you are being treated at a hospital, go to the hospital's chief financial officer (rather than discussing your dispute with the collection office, which really has no authority to reduce or modify bills.)

If you still feel dissatisfied, contact the state or local agency that licenses hospitals or medical professionals. Many states have a dispute processing center for just this problem.

Pay what you think is fair and justified, recognizing the risk that the health-care provider may sue you for the rest. In court, of course, you can require the provider to justify his billings, and ask to have your records produced.

(You cannot refuse payment simply because you have not been cured: neither doctors nor hospitals warrant that their treatment will cure. Charges are based on the time spent in treatment.)

Contact your local office of Medicare or Medicaid and ask for a listing of reasonable prices charged locally for the specific services you received. Such lists are also maintained by other health insurers.

Health Insurance

For most people, health insurance is an absolute necessity. Without it the costs of unexpected medical bills can devastate a family's budget. But there is an infinite variety of health plans available for purchase, and you should be careful to get the coverage best suited to your needs and circumstances.

There are various levels of premium payments. The basic coverage generally pertains to a certain percentage of hospital and medical costs incurred by either you or your family. But not all policies are family-coverage plans—so read the policy statements carefully to see who is covered and how reimbursements are made. Some policies pay the doctor or provider directly; others reimburse you for expenses.

Other policies cover greater percentages of your hospital bill, and may also cover you and your family for dental care, eye care, and the like. Because such policies are more comprehensive, they are more expensive. Do not assume that you are covered for anything. Read the policy carefully before you purchase it. You might also join a clinic or Health Maintenance Organization.

Your state's insurance commissioner should be able to answer questions about local health insurers.

Some payments go directly to the doctor. Assignments are payments that the doctor or other health-care provider agrees to accept directly from the health insurer—in full satisfaction of your bill. For instance, if the insurance company will pay 80 percent of your care bill, you can ask your doctor if he will accept this 80 percent in full payment of your claim; if he does, you will owe him nothing further. Many doctors will agree to such an arrangement to encourage confidence and good will in their patients, as well as to assure prompt payment.

The government often helps. Almost all states have some type of medical assistance programs to help individuals unable to afford health insurance themselves. All states participate in Medicaid—the health-care system run by the federal government. You can find out whether you are qualified for Medicaid by contacting your local office; look up "Medicaid" in your telephone directory.

Medicare is a federally funded and administered program that pays for certain items of health care for persons over sixty-five, or persons with certain disabilities. For more information about Medicare (and the optional premium policy under

Medicare B), contact the Health Care Financing Administration or Social Security office in your area.

The Right to Die

Some states have legislated a right to die. In some states critically ill people are granted the option of having life-sustaining procedures withheld or removed if they are in a coma and have a minimal chance of recovering. Life-sustaining treatment is that which is necessary, not to cure an individual, but merely to keep him technically alive through mechanical and chemical means. The main issue is whether *doctors* can refuse treatment to such an individual: in some jurisdictions, doctors can be criminally charged and subject to professional discipline if they allow such patients to be taken off life-sustaining treatments.

In states that allow a right to die, the patient or his guardian must sign a specific document to allow or prohibit any treatment. When a guardian is involved, the restrictions are stringent. To fully understand the procedures that exist in your state, call your health agency, board of medical examiners, or doctor.

Malpractice Suits

Medical malpractice is not easy to prove. It might be easier to understand what is *not* medical malpractice. Medical malpractice is not your right to be cured. Doctors do not have a duty to cure patients; therefore they cannot be sued for failure to cure. A physician is generally held to the standard of care and skill expected of a reasonably prudent doctor in the geographic area where he practices, under similar circumstances. If a specialist is involved, the standard of care reasonably to be expected of a specialist in that field (generally a higher standard of care) is applied. If the doctor does not perform up to that subjectively defined standard, and you have been damaged as a result, you can bring suit against him for your damages. Some states have voluntary arbitration procedures in these cases; one (Maryland) requires arbitration of all claims over $5,000.

The same rules apply to other health-care providers, like medical laboratories or hospitals.

You usually need a lawyer for a malpractice suit. This is because of the complexities of medical malpractice and the different standards that apply from state to state. Medical malpractice cases are difficult to prove, and are sometimes even more difficult because doctors are often extremely reluctant to testify against a fellow doctor in regard to breaches of the local standard of care.

In addition, there are usually questions involving specific *statutes of limitations*—how long a period of time you have in which to bring a suit—on which a lawyer should be consulted, particularly whether the time runs from the date that it was reasonable to have discovered it.

There is a wealth of information available about representing yourself in health matters. For starters, see Bibliography under "Health Matters."

11

Wills and Probate

When there's a will there's a way.
—George Bernard Shaw
FANNY'S FIRST PLAY

DISTRIBUTING the assets of an estate can be a complex legal experience. Long ago, laws were adopted to spell out the rules for dividing property when one died *intestate* (without a will). More recently the laws have been made even more complicated by the government, in its efforts to share in the spoils. Creditors have always wanted to be paid off as well. The law has thus developed a pecking order for the proceeds of an estate where there is no will—with the heirs usually at the bottom.

There are several reasons to have a will. Most important, if you don't state your desires as to how much your spouse should get (beyond the minimum the law requires), the law will make the decision for you—and what the law provides may not coincide with your wishes. And the law never provides for small gifts to friends or to other than immediate relatives. You should also remember that many provisions, such as posting a bond for the executor or appointing special guardians for your minor children, can be avoided if you state in your will that you want to eliminate them. If you don't have a will, these provisions, or "protections," are mandatory, and may cost your heirs both time and money. But the fact that you need a will doesn't mean that in most cases you can't draft one yourself, with perhaps a quick perusal by a lawyer at the end.

Your estate includes everything of monetary value or personal significance. Primarily your estate is your home and other real estate; bank accounts, cars, silver, valuable jewelry and dishes, and other personal property; personal papers; hobby collections and art objects; investment portfolio; and certain rights under your pension plans. Almost all adults have a personal estate. Even housewives who have never worked outside the home have estates if title or any property or bank account is in their own name, or if they have inherited anything of value.

Intestate estates are divided according to local law. Persons who die without a valid will are said to have died intestate. Their estates are distributed in accordance with the statutory laws of intestate succession for the state in which they were domiciled at the time of their death. In short, people who die without a valid will allow a state legislature (rather than themselves) to determine how to distribute their estate.

Intestate laws vary from state to state. Usually the surviving spouse will receive from one third to one half of the estate, with the balance going to the children (if any), to the surviving parents, or to brothers and sisters and other kin. The result may be a distribution completely at variance with the wishes of the decedent and the needs of those dependent upon the estate.

Even if the distribution by intestate succession is the same as the decedent would have wished, there are still advantages to having a will. Intestate procedures are generally more cumbersome, time-consuming, and expensive than those involved in the probate (approval) of a will. A court-appointed personal representative is required to post a bond to assure honest performance. In a will, the testator (one who makes the will) can appoint his or her own choice of personal representative, determine the guardianship of any children, and waive (give up) the expensive requirement of posting a bond.

Keep in mind also that a court-appointed personal representative must often file petitions and secure court approval before taking even the most sensible and necessary actions on behalf of the estate; personal representatives appointed by a will are not subject to such burdens as long as they act reasonably and prudently.

You can make your own will without hiring a lawyer. Under certain circumstances a reasonably intelligent person can write a will as well as many attorneys.

If your estate is small, does not involve complicated holdings, and if you don't expect any of your heirs to be disappointed enough over their share of the distribution to make a fuss, it can be a relatively easy matter to draw up your own will. If, on the other hand, your estate could benefit from tax planning, or if there are ex-spouses, stepchildren, or children from a prior marriage, you would be better off having a good attorney draft your will. Likewise, if you are considering a trust, or leaving your estate to your grandchildren rather than your children, or if you can foresee that your intended distribution might create a stir among your heirs, you should definitely hire an attorney.

A simple estate is one which consists primarily of life insurance payable to a first beneficiary, backed by a second beneficiary; bank accounts with rights of survivorship; a house and car held as community property (or in a joint tenancy with rights of survivorship, or as a tenancy by the entirety); and furniture and other personal property of negligible monetary value.

Tenancy by the entirety is the particular form of ownership allowed only to married couples. It means that each owns an undivided half of the property, and if one owner dies, the surviving spouse then owns the whole thing. It is just like a joint tenancy except that neither spouse can sell his or her share without permission of the other. The major difference between a joint tenancy and a tenancy by the entirety is that the former can be changed by either spouse during his or her lifetime; the latter can be terminated only by death, divorce, or mutual agreement. Any form of ownership may be stated on a deed or other type of title to property, as well as in a separate document.

Determine how large your estate is before you decide to hire a lawyer. If the total value of your estate (including the equity you have in your house) should exceed the amount exempt from federal estate and gift taxes, hire an attorney experienced in estate planning. Because an estate of this size is subject to federal estate and gift taxes, the services of a knowledgeable attorney could mean substantial savings in tax dollars far outweighing the legal fees charged.

Similarly, if there are children from former marriages or stepchildren, advice from an experienced lawyer could prevent family dissent and tension.

Finally, if you are interested in creating a trust (where ownership of certain property or funds is given to one party who must act for the benefit of other designated parties), or in giving a life estate to one person regarding certain property (so that upon his or her death ownership of the property would automatically transfer to some other designated person), or any other scheme that might be complicated or controversial, the drafting of such provisions should be attempted only by a competent lawyer.

Every will should include certain items. Even simple wills should contain at least the following:

1. The full name and permanent address of the testator
2. A declaration that this document is the testator's last will and testament, and revokes all former wills and codicils (written amendments)
3. A brief description of all the real and personal property which the testator wishes to bequeath

4. Specific *bequests* (gifts of personal property), *devices* (gifts of real property), and *legacies* (gifts of sums of money), including gifts to charities or friends
5. Where the residue of the estate should go (with several alternatives)
6. The names of guardians for one's minor children upon death of both parents
7. Appointment of a personal representative to handle the probate of the estate (often the surviving spouse)
8. An express statement that it is the testator's intent that the state-imposed bond requirement be waived for the personal representative
9. Establishment of trusts, when such are desired (including mention of the general powers of the trustee; special instructions as to the management of the trust; and naming the person or corporation who should act as the trustee and the persons who should be the beneficiaries; giving instructions as to where the income from the trust is to be channeled and to whom the principal or corpus of the trust is to be eventually distributed; and when such distribution is to take place)
10. The signature of the testator at the very end of the provisions (in the presence of witnesses)
11. Signatures of the witnesses after the testator's signature, along with an attestation clause (such as: "The foregoing instrument was at the date thereof signed, published, and declared by the said [testator's name] as and for his last will and testament in the joint presence of us, who, at his request and in his presence, and in the presence of each other, havè subscribed our names as witnesses")
12. The date that the signatures were affixed
13. The witnesses' permanent addresses

Oral wills are generally not valid. A few states have laws which allow oral wills in certain very limited situations (for example, where the will was made during the testator's last sickness). In these circumstances two (in some states, three) people must have been requested by the testator to bear witness to the contents of his will, and they all must have heard the contents of the will at the same time in each other's presence. In addition, such witnesses must have reduced their testimony of what they heard into writing within a certain number of days, and the resulting will must be offered for probate within a certain number of months afterward. Even then, the amount and kinds of property which can pass by oral will is usually limited.

Similarly, in most jurisdictions the oral wills of soldiers in active military service and of sailors at sea are privileged—that is, their verbal (or unattested written) wills are capable of passing their personal property.

If there is any dispute as to the validity of a will (oral or written), you should consult an attorney.

Handwritten wills are valid. By statute in various states, *holographic wills* (those that are handwritten, dated, and signed by the testator) are valid without attestation or the other formalities of execution. In the other states, however, formal attestation is required regardless of whether the will is handwritten, typed, or printed. And some states will recognize a will that is valid according to the laws of the jurisdiction in which it was made. There is nothing that requires a will to be typewritten, so long as the other formalities are met.

Nineteen states currently allow unattested holographic wills. They are Arizona, Arkansas, California, Idaho, Kentucky, Louisiana, Mississippi, Montana, Nevada, North Carolina, North Dakota, Oklahoma, South Dakota, Tennessee, Texas, Utah, Virginia, West Virginia, and Wyoming.

Making a proper will means following certain steps. First, you should select as your witnesses stable adults who have no direct or indirect interest in your estate. This means that your beneficiaries, heirs, personal administrators, and trustees, as well as those persons' spouses, should not witness your will. Wills executed in Connecticut, Georgia, Maine, Massachusetts, New Hampshire, South Carolina, and Vermont must have at least three witnesses. In all other states except Louisiana, the attestation of only two witnesses is sufficient. (The laws of Louisiana are heavily influenced by the French civil law, rather than the British common law which forms the legal basis of the other states. Residents of Louisiana should consult a lawyer in making wills.) To be safe, have three witnesses sign your will.

Second, you should personally sign and date the very bottom of the will. Any provisions added after the signature of the testator will not be considered by the probate court, and may possibly invalidate the entire will.

Third, the witnesses should sign the will under an attestation clause. Some states demand that witnesses be in each other's presence when they sign, so this is the better practice. The witnesses do not have to read any of the will. They need only be able to testify that the testator signed the will in their presence, declared it to be his last will, requested the proper number of witnesses to attest the execution of the document as a will, and that they did so. The witnesses' addresses should also be noted in the will.

Finally, it is a good idea for both the testator and the witnesses to initial or sign each individual page of the will (which should also be numbered), to discourage later attempts at substituting pages. After all that is done, be sure there is at least one extra copy that is signed and attested.

Certain legal requirements must be met before a probate court will validate a will. The testator must have been of legal age (generally eighteen years old), mentally competent, and not acting under any undue influence at the time of making the will. He must have had the intention to make a will. He must not have revoked it prior to his death. The specific provisions of the will must not offend any statutory requirements of the state in which it was executed, or offend public policy (in the opinion of the probate court). Finally, the will must not have been "revoked by law" because of significant changes in the circumstances of the testator which occurred since the time of the will's execution (for example, marriage, divorce, birth of a child, or perhaps the death of the principal beneficiary).

Public policy might be offended if, for example, a testator left all his property to an animal and none to his wife. Likewise, in most states you can't disinherit a spouse.

You cannot later change your will by crossing out or erasing provisions. Never try to change an operative will (one that has been signed and witnessed) by erasing or crossing out provisions or names or amounts. Attempts to do so will be considered invalid because of the lack of the proper formalities of execution. Most probate courts disdain attempts to alter the will in such an informal manner, and may invalidate the whole document.

You do not have to make a new will every time you want to change a provision. A new will is not necessary every time a change is desired. By use of a codicil, a testator can make limited changes without having to revoke and rewrite the entire will. A *codicil* is a supplement or amendment adding to, deleting from, or modifying the terms of a will. In order for it to be valid, it must be executed with the same formalities as a will. It should specifically identify the will to which it should be attached, mention previous codicils if any, and affirm those portions of the will and former codicils that it does not seek to modify.

Consider changing your will when there is a major change in your life. The necessity or desirability of a codicil (or even a new will) should be considered any time there is a change in the testator's life, such as the birth of a child; marriage, divorce, or the death of a spouse; any increase or change in the value or nature of his property, or when a selected personal representative or trustee dies or otherwise becomes unable to serve.

Revocation of an existing will or codicil should always be accompanied by the execution of a new will or codicil. Even if you decide to have your estate distributed by intestate succession, it is still wise formally to revoke the will and indicate your preference for intestacy. Tearing or burning a will with the intent to revoke it may be a legally effective method of revocation, but when done in the privacy of one's home the gesture may go unrecognized. The probate court may consider the destroyed will as being lost and accept a carbon copy provided by the drafting attorney (or even one of the beneficiaries) in substitution. In short, if a will is to be revoked without a simultaneous replacement, there should be a paper where the will itself would have been, affirming the revocation.

Do not keep your will in a safe-deposit box. Your most recent will should be clearly marked as such, and kept wherever you keep important documents in your home. Your spouse and children should be told of its location. Many lawyers think it is better *not* to keep your will in a safe-deposit box—which is temporarily sealed in many areas when the bank is notified of death and may thus be less convenient than a location in your home. Some people ask their lawyers to keep the original in their office safe, or to file it in court.

Probate is not always necessary. Probate is the process by which a will is proved to the proper authorities (usually a probate court). To the extent that property is held in joint tenancy, it automatically transfers to the survivor upon the death of one tenant, and therefore eliminates the necessity of probate (although not necessarily the necessity for paying estate taxes). Note, however, that under the Economic Recovery Act of 1981, all assets can be passed tax-free to a surviving spouse. Note also that a bequest which blindly passes all assets to the spouse will not accomplish the optimum tax-saving available; an automatic unlimited gift wastes the shelter provided by the federal estate and gift tax laws. This makes no difference, of course, unless your estate is quite large. (See the latest edition of *How to Avoid Probate*, by Norman F. Dacey.)

Even when there is probate, a lawyer is not always required. If the remainder of the estate involves a relatively small amount of money, and no one is contesting the provisions of the will, a lawyer is often not necessary. A designated personal representative can usually obtain the necessary legal forms to be filled out from the clerk's office handling probate matters. These papers should include a *petition for probate/request for letters testamentary*; a statement from the personal representative consenting to appointment, notice of appointment and notice to creditors; appraiser's reports; and requests for bond where necessary. Once the court confirms the appointment of the personal representative, it will issue *letters testamentary*, a document which gives the personal representative permission to transact any matters on behalf of the deceased's estate.

The personal representative (executor) has specific responsibilities. Initially, the personal representative should submit any will that has been found to the probate court. Ultimately, the personal representative is responsible for gathering all the assets and investing, disposing of, or preserving them; paying all valid debts from these assets; and then distributing the remainder as the testator directed (if there was a valid will) or according to the law of intestate succession (if there was no valid will). The personal representative is also responsible for the preparation and filing of any federal estate tax return, any state inheritance tax returns, the fiduciary tax return, and any income tax returns required as a result of the death, and for paying those taxes from the assets of the estate. This must be done within the legal time limit and before final distribution of the estate. All these actions are done under the supervision of the probate court and are part of what is called "probating a will."

Your Work

12

Employees' Rights

O, how full of briers is this working-day world.
—Shakespeare, As You Like It

For a variety of reasons, the law in the field of employment is more stacked against the average person than in almost any other area. This has two important consequences. First, an employee can normally obtain the best results, not by consorting with lawyers, but by organizing with other employees to persuade the employer to grant concessions. Second, because of the numerous procedural pitfalls which line the path to justice in this area, an employee is often best advised to use remedies for which lawyers, such as government attorneys, can be obtained free of charge.

Knowing your legal rights, of course, minimizes your reliance on any lawyers at all.

Your rights begin when you apply for a job. Often the first contact you have with a prospective employer is through his advertisements. Under federal and many state laws, employers are not permitted to place notices in a discriminatory way. For example, they cannot advertise for employees of a particular race, color, national origin, religion, or sex (or for an employee who is *not* a member of such a group), unless those qualifica-

111

tions are considered necessary to perform a specific job. (If an employer wanted a women's room attendant, he could legally require that she be female. This exception is called a "bona fide occupational qualification.")

Certain kinds of discrimination are permitted. As long as federal or state laws do not prohibit a particular personal trait from being discriminated against (or from being required by an employer as a prerequisite to employment), such discrimination is allowable. For example, if an employer wants all his employees to have brown eyes, he can legally discriminate against people with blue eyes, provided that the effect is not prohibited by state or federal law and does not exclude from consideration a protected class of persons. An employer might even ask if you are married—if, for example, he does not want a single person to manage a computer-dating service. (Marital status questions must be job-related.)

Employment agencies are also restricted. If you work through an employment agency in trying to find a job, understand that agencies also are prohibited from discriminating in an unlawful manner in their advertising, their practices, or in any agreements made with prospective employers.

You should inquire about the fee to be paid to the agency for finding you a job, particularly about whether it is to be paid by you or the employer. The fee may be payable even if you don't stay with the employer. States generally establish the maximum fees which can be charged and the conditions under which these fees may be imposed. If in doubt, check with your state's labor commissioner or similar agency.

An employer may check your background and credit. Generally, employers are permitted to make reasonably thorough background checks on prospective employees, as long as the information sought is related to the position being applied for. The degree to which an investigation may go likewise depends upon the job in question. A background check for a bank teller, for example, would be more stringent than that for an assembly-line worker.

The investigation may not be used as a means to unlawfully discriminate against you.

An employer may also check your credit rating, but very strict guidelines are set under the Federal Credit Reporting Act and the credit reporting acts of some states. If you are turned down for employment, you are entitled to know the name of the agency that supplied a credit report. If the federal act is violated, the employer is subject to both civil and criminal penalties, and you may pursue him for both actual and punitive damages, as well as for attorney fees.

An employer may test you. Generally an employer can use any "professionally developed ability test" as long as that test does not discriminate against your race, color, religion, sex, or national origin. Again, such tests must be job-related. If you feel that a test was discriminatory or not job-related, contact your state labor commissioner or your local office of the federal Equal Employment Opportunity Commission (EEOC).

Do not lie on an employment application. Remember that any incorrect or false statement in an employment application is sufficient grounds not to hire you—or to fire you if the employer finds out later—not because of what your answers were or should have been, but because the answers were false.

Many states prohibit the use of a lie detector or polygraph test in any connection with employment activities.

Check with your state labor department or with your local union for more information.

You should probably sign any waivers or releases requested to allow distribution of information from your former employer. Employers who ask for such waivers usually intend to use them. Although you certainly may refuse to sign them, if you don't get the job, the employer can reasonably claim it was because you were uncooperative or were trying to hide something in your past. The employer may lawfully not hire you, and you probably won't have any recourse against him (unless, of course, you can show that the request was discriminatory).

An employer can require medical examinations. If it is necessary to assess your capability to perform job-related functions, a medical examination can be required. Handicapped people are protected by the Federal Rehabilitation Act of 1973 or similar state statutes prohibiting employment discrimination based on physical handicap.

An employer can ask for certain information which you might feel discriminates. Employers may ask for discriminatory information if it is used solely for reporting to government agencies which request various data for such things as employment-practice programs. The information may not, however, be used for hiring purposes, and this should be made clear by the employer.

You cannot be discriminated against because of your age. Under the federal Age Discrimination Act an employer is prohibited from arbitrarily discriminating against you on account of your age if you are between forty and seventy. Those covered by this act are private employers with twenty or more employees, federal or state governments (regardless of the number of employees), employment agencies, and labor organizations with twenty-five or more members. If you feel that you have been discriminated against because of your age, contact your local office of the Equal Employment Opportunity Commission (EEOC).

Some states have their own age discrimination laws. Check with your state labor commissioner for information.

Vietnam veterans are especially protected. Under the federal Vietnam Era Veterans' Readjustment Assistance Act of 1974, the fact that you are a veteran cannot be held against you during the first four years after your discharge. If a veteran has 30 percent or more disability, he can be protected throughout his working life. Information about this program, and which employers are covered under it, can be obtained from the Veterans Administration, or from your local office of the federal Department of Labor.

Your rights as an employee depend on a variety of circumstances. It all depends on who you are, where you work, whom you work for, what type of work you are doing, and what additional rights are in your contract. If you work for a private employer and you are not represented by a union, your relationship with your employer is more under his control. Nevertheless, he is still subject to various state laws, and if he employs more than a certain number of people (specified by statute), has government contracts, or his business is in interstate commerce, he may also be subject to various federal laws. Statutes (both federal and state, and in some cases, even city and county) may regulate your wages and hours, assure you of nondiscriminatory treatment in employment, promotion, and pay, and guarantee a safe work environment and pension rights. Unions (including those for government employees) often add to these basic rights by gaining employer concessions for medical and sick benefits, pensions, grievance procedures, strike clauses, and the right not to be fired except for just cause.

Even if you don't belong to a union, you have basic rights. Assuming that you work for a small company, you have rights specified by the state law (usually the right to work in a safe environment, for a minimum wage, and for a maximum number of hours), and those especially contracted for. The last are the trickiest, because many employment "contracts" are unwritten agreements which can be terminated at the will of either party. This type of contract generally arises when, after an interview, you and the employer "shake hands" on your "agreement" to accept the job, based on the salary and benefits that you have discussed. The terms of your contract may be listed in a letter to you from your employer, but most often they are merely evidenced by the wages you are paid and the benefits you receive or have been promised. Because very little has been committed to writing, many rights or benefits to which your employer may have agreed orally may be difficult to secure if he later chooses to ignore or deny them. Thus, the best advice is to get as much in writing as you can, and ask questions before problems arise.

If you work for a larger company, you might receive a manual explaining what is required of you as an employee, and what benefits you are due in return. Many employers go so far as to require that you sign a form indicating you have read and agreed to the information in the manual. This may create an agreement binding on both you and the company, depending on state law. Any disputes that might arise can probably be decided under the manual, so read it carefully.

In addition, some courts have held that public policy demands that employment contracts include an implicit, unwritten term of "good faith and fair dealing" toward employees, and have forbidden companies from firing employees for improper reasons (such as filing workmen's compensation claims or refusing to cover up illegal activities).

Union contracts are generally comprehensive. If you belong to a union, your rights are generally at least as good as if you were not represented by a union. In addition, the union has negotiated a written contract covering your employment, which often gives you greater protection. You should have a copy of the contract, so that you will know exactly what your rights are. Union contracts usually don't specify your personal rate of pay, but may place you in a class of employees with a specified pay scale based on the number of years on the job and the type of work you do. Wage and salary increases are also specified, as well as health benefits and pension plans.

Union contracts also generally include a grievance procedure, so that you can complain through the union to your employer if, for example, the terms of the contract regarding break time or sick leave are not being met. In fact, the contractually established grievance procedures must ordinarily be followed whenever you assert your contractual rights. You can resort to court actions, however, if you think the union is acting capriciously or arbitrarily, or otherwise not fairly representing you with regard to your complaint. To do so, however, you may have to take your complaint to court quickly after losing a grievance or learning of the union's improper conduct, but such actions are difficult to win.

Your union membership cannot be restricted. If you belong to a union, or you want to organize a union among the workers in your company, you have certain rights under federal laws. These statutes protect the right to organize, the right to participate in union activities, and the right *not* to be represented if a majority of your fellow employees agree.

You also have a right to vote in union elections without management (or union) interference, and to engage in activities with other employees—through a union, or independently—for mutual aid, benefit, or protection. Your employer cannot interfere with or discriminate against employees who exercise such rights. Neither can employers discriminate against anyone who files a complaint with the National Labor Relations Board (NLRB), which protects employees whose rights have been infringed. You are equally protected against unfair restraints placed upon you by unions, as well as by employers.

Enforcing National Labor Relations Act rights is not necessarily complicated. If you feel you are not being treated fairly by an employer or union, you must first file a charge with the NLRB stating an unfair labor practice. Charges must be filed with the NLRB within six months of the alleged violation. The charge can be filed in the NLRB's regional offices (look in the phone book, under U.S. Government). If the NLRB agrees that your employer or union is subject to NLRA, and that you are a covered employee (i.e., not an employee of the federal or state government, not a supervisor, or not subject to other federal laws like the Railway Labor Act, which covers rail and airline employees), it will investigate your charge.

You can get a charge form from your regional NLRB office. The form must be truthfully filled in, sworn to or affirmed under oath, and filed. (Your union can also file a charge on your behalf.) The other party will be notified of your complaint, and an investigation will be undertaken by the regional office to determine whether an unfair labor practice has occurred. If the NLRB concludes that a violation has occurred, it will issue a complaint. Even if they conclude that a violation has not occurred, you cannot be fired for filing a complaint in good faith.

If the regional office concludes that your charge lacks merit, you can appeal to the NLRB's Office of Appeals in Washington which can direct that a complaint be issued. Then a hearing will be held before an administrative law judge who will issue proposed findings, which are then reviewed by the NLRB in Washington. If an unfair labor practice is found, the Board will issue an appropriate order—for example, one which will require immediate corrective action, including back pay if appropriate.

Although the NLRB's regional legal staff will represent you in the matter, you should nevertheless be active in preparation of your case. You may also have your own lawyer if you wish.

If the union or employer fails to obey the Board's order, the NLRB will seek to enforce it in a federal court.

Complaining to EEOC is similarly uncomplicated. If you feel that you have been discriminated against in employment because of your race, color, religion, sex, or national origin, take your complaint to your local EEOC office within 180 days of the discriminatory act. In many areas, the EEOC has designated specific state offices to handle such complaints.

The procedure is similar to that followed with the NLRB. You must fill out a complaint form, stating how you feel you have been discriminated against. The EEOC will investigate your complaint. If it finds merit, it may order a hearing. If a hearing is ordered, the employer will be asked to justify his conduct in reference to the complaint. Initially, the EEOC acts as an intermediary with your employer, but if an act is considered discriminatory, it pursues the employer for you as if it were your counsel.

If the EEOC determines that your complaint lacks merit, it will be dismissed and your employer will be so informed. In this case, or where the EEOC has simply been unable to process your claim within 180 days, you are entitled to receive a Right to Sue letter. You will then have ninety days in which to file an action for discrimination in a Federal District Court, or risk losing your action completely. (More detailed instructions can easily be obtained through your local EEOC office.)

Preparation is important. You may decide to retain counsel to assist you in organizing your complaint, or you may proceed yourself. Either way, the key to success is good preparation. Find others who are aware of the possible discrimination at work, and ask them to corroborate your complaint. Their written statements should be sworn before a notary public; you can get the necessary format from the EEOC (or NLRB) office.

Before you prepare your case, make certain that you are covered under the law. This may be done by asking the information officer at the NLRB or EEOC. You might find several books in your public library (or through your union office) to assist you in understanding the intricacies of labor law. Do not hesitate to see a lawyer if you are unable to understand the law or what you can do to protect your rights:

if you eventually win your EEOC case, you will be awarded attorney fees. This does not apply in NLRB cases, however.

Check the state law, too. As long as state regulations have not been displaced by federal law, states may control employer-employee relationships, or judge the fairness of employee discharges under common-law or public-policy principles.

States often have their own laws for minimum wages and overtime, maximum hours, the health and safety of the work environment (e.g., noise, dust, and fume levels, or exposure to toxic chemicals and asbestos), and child employment. Many federal laws exist in these areas also, but state laws that are more stringent are also enforceable. For example, many states have their own prohibitions against sexual harassment in the workplace.

Other employee rights are protected not by statute but by state courts applying "public policy." For example, a court may enjoin a discharge if it came about because the employee wished to be a jury member, voted in a manner contrary to his or her employer's wishes, or refused to do something illegal, unethical, or dishonest—even for reporting a fellow employee to a supervisor or to a governmental authority for wrongful acts. Such "whistle-blowing" is protected by statute in a number of states and if you are a federal employee.

Public servants are sometimes more vulnerable, and sometimes better off. State employees are generally not covered by federal statutes, and are sometimes not even protected by state laws that apply to private employers. This is due to the unique role of the state as both an employer and a regulator. Unlike private employees, government workers receive the full protection of persons under the state and federal constitutions, and an employment contract written by the state cannot be abridged by state law.

Many government employees belong to unions, receiving the benefits and protection afforded them in the union contract, but many government unions are prohibited from striking.

For more information about rights of state employees, check with your personnel commissioner or union representative. Federal employees are regulated by the policies of the Office of Personnel Management, and their unions come under the jurisdiction of the Federal Labor Relations Authority.

13

Starting a Business

Anybody can start something.
—John A. Shedd, SALT FROM MY ATTIC

SMALL businesses are an important facet of the economic system—and the courage and hope that go into starting one are integral parts of the American psyche. There are close to 5 million small firms in this country, representing the great majority of all business concerns and employing over half the nation's workers. New businesses start (and many fledgling ones fail) every day. Would-be entrepreneurs need not have a lawyer to begin.

A business can be operated as a sole proprietorship, partnership (general or limited), a joint venture, or corporation.

A *sole proprietorship* exists when the person operating a business goes it alone. He is the boss, although the authority to make decisions can be delegated to an employee. The sole proprietor is personally responsible for all debts and losses incurred by the business. Of course, the sole proprietor is entitled to all the profits as well. Because he is on his own, the laws concerning sole proprietors are similar to those concerning any individual. This chapter will thus deal primarily with partnerships and corporations, although most laws (e.g., minimum-wage regulations) apply regardless of the form of organization.

Partnerships

Partners share in profits and losses. A voluntary association between two or more persons, who intend to share profits (and losses) from the operation of a business, is a *partnership*. The partners' intentions and expectations should be set out in a written partnership agreement, but partnerships can and do exist which are based on purely oral agreements, and can even arise solely out of the acts of the parties toward themselves and others. The primary advantage of a partnership is to exploit the idea that "two heads are better than one"—to generate ideas, efforts, and income.

There are several drawbacks to operating a business as a partnership. One major disadvantage of an ordinary partnership is the unlimited personal liability of each of the individual partners for the firm's debts and losses. *Limited* partners (and owners of a corporation) can restrict their potential loss to their capital investment—and no more. Another disadvantage is that one partner's act can bind the partnership: the other partners are fully liable for one of their member's mistakes. Moreover, if the partnership incurs debts and there are not sufficient assets in the firm to pay for them, each partner is individually liable. Creditors can even choose which partner to proceed against, because the debts do not have to be allocated proportionately.

The partners are not always bound by every act of one partner. When one partner's acts are obviously not in the ordinary course of the business, the other partners are not bound. For example, if your partner in the shoe-repair business takes a trip to Hawaii "to look for customers," you aren't required to pay for his airplane ticket. Likewise, when the partner in fact has no authority to act for the partnership in a particular matter *and* the third party with whom he is dealing knows about this limitation, the partner's acts are not binding.

You do not need a lawyer to create a partnership. But keep in mind that the services of a knowledgeable attorney or certified public accountant might be a sound business expense. Partnership agreements and similar business contracts are not mere formalities drafted for show or to impress potential creditors. They should be useful documents, outlining the genuine expectations of the parties as to how the business should be created, operated, and dissolved.

A good lawyer could be invaluable in discussing such areas as profit and loss sharing; tax planning; and the operational responsibilities of the parties. If you and your partners do not have a clear understanding regarding these matters, you are headed for trouble. (Note that an unsigned or unwritten understanding is not illegal—it is just useless for most purposes.)

Various items should be included in a partnership agreement. Every ordinary partnership agreement should contain at least the following:

1. The name and address of the business
2. The purpose of the partnership
3. The date the partnership is to become effective (and, if known, the date it will expire)
4. The names and addresses of the partners
5. How profits and losses are to be shared
6. The capital (money, services, supplies or equipment) each partner is contributing
7. The salaries or rights to withdraw capital to be allowed to each partner
8. How much time each partner is expected to devote to the business
9. The authority of each partner in operating the business (especially the division of decision making, the power to

sign checks, to make loans, to buy goods, or to enter
into contracts and leases)
10. How and by whom the business is to be managed
11. Who is responsible for accounting and the preparation
of financial statements
12. A provision for the dissolution of the partnership and the
right to continue the business should a partner withdraw
13. How any profits or surplus should be distributed upon
dissolution
14. A provision for continuing the business upon the death
or insanity of a partner (if this should be the intention
of the partners), and whether or not the legal representative of an incapacitated or deceased partner should
have access to books and records of the firm

Partnerships don't last forever. Unless the partnership agreement otherwise provides, the partnership automatically ends if
a partner dies, becomes insane, or is no longer competent. If
one of the partners wants to retire, or if another person wishes
to join the partnership, the old agreement is dissolved, and a
new one is created with the consent of the new partners. When
a partner retires, he usually remains liable to creditors for the
debts of the partnership incurred prior to his retirement. The
incoming partner is not liable unless he assumes such an obligation.

**Liabilities of a dissolved partnership are distributed according
to a prescribed order.** When a partnership is formally dissolved, liabilities of the business are paid out of its assets in the
following order:

1. Those due to creditors other than partners
2. Those due to partners for loans or other debts from the
firm to them (a partner's capital investment is not considered a debt fitting into this category)
3. Those due to partners for their share of the capital
investment and the profits

A limited partner differs from a general or ordinary partner.
Even a limited partnership requires at least one general partner, that is, one whose liability for the debts of the partnership
is unlimited. The rest of the partners can be limited partners. A
limited partner is not personally bound by the obligations of
the partnership beyond his specific investment of capital. Once
that capital contribution has been used to pay creditors, the
limited partner has no further obligations, either to the
creditors or to the other partners. Such a limitation is obviously
a valuable protection, and it can be obtained only by complying with the state's partnership law. Creditors would be wise to
check beforehand to find out who in the partnership will be responsible for the debts it incurs. This can be accomplished by
contacting the state agency in charge of limited partnerships
(call the general information number listed in your telephone
book under "State Government"). If no literature is available,
you may need to hire an attorney for proper advice. Remember,
strict compliance is essential. Of course, some lenders will
make a loan to a limited partnership only if the limited partners agree to become personally liable for debts the partnership can't pay. There's nothing improper about such a request
—it's a matter of business judgment whether the limited partners will agree.

**Various items should be included in a limited partnership
agreement.** A limited partnership agreement, in compliance
with the Uniform Limited Partnership Act (or applicable state
law, if it differs), should include at least the following:

1. The name of the partnership
2. The nature of the business
3. The location of the principal place of business
4. The name and address of each general or limited partner
5. The term of the partnership
6. The amount of cash or value of other property contributed by each limited partner (a limited partner may

contribute cash or property as his capital contribution, but not services)

7. The subsequent contributions, if any, to be made by each limited partner and when they are to be made
8. Whether any contribution of each limited partner is to be returned and if so under what conditions
9. The share of the profits each limited partner shall receive
10. The right to admit additional limited or general partners
11. Any priorities given to one or more limited partners over other limited partners
12. The right of any remaining general partners to continue the business on the death, retirement, or insanity of a general partner
13. The right, if any, of a limited partner to receive property instead of cash in return for his contribution
14. The right, if any and under what conditions, of a limited partner to substitute another in his place

A joint venture differs little from a partnership. When two or more persons get together to complete a single business transaction—rather than establish and operate a continuous business together—it is more accurately termed a joint venture. It has most of the attributes of a partnership, and so a partnership type of agreement should be drafted and signed by the parties involved. Even when a single transaction rather than a continuous business is involved, it is best to put in writing the intentions of the parties.

Corporations

A corporation is an artificial legal entity. It is created under the authority of state, or in some cases federal, law, and has the legal powers to do anything an individual or partnership can do: operate a business, lend and borrow money, own property, sue and be sued.

A single individual can own a corporation. A business operated as a corporation can be formed and owned by a single person or many individuals or even other corporations or partnerships. The number of owners is irrelevant since the law regards the corporation itself as having a personality and existence distinct from that of its shareholders. In fact, corporations are considered to have the attribute of *perpetual succession*. This means that a corporation is thought to continually exist, ever the same, despite the change of the individuals who own it. These individuals are known as the stockholders or shareholders because they have contributed capital (anything of value: money, property, equipment, services, and the like) to the corporation in exchange for shares of the corporation's stock.

Why incorporate? The great advantage to creating a corporation is that its owners (i.e., the stockholders) have only limited liability for debts and losses. The corporation itself is responsible for its financial status; it is considered separate and distinct from its owners. While the owners recover profits in proportion to the number of shares of stock they own, their losses are limited to their capital investment, that is, the money and property they contributed in exchange for a share in the business. In contrast, those operating a sole proprietorship or as partners are liable to the full extent of their assets including their personal property. Thus, a corporation is the most protective form of business. But like limited partnerships, small corporations may be able to obtain certain loans only if their principal owners give the lender a personal promise (guarantee) of repayment.

A second advantage to operating a business as a corporation is that corporate earnings are taxed at a lower rate than individual earnings. But the tax consequences of incorporation are tricky, and it would be best to consult a lawyer or accountant.

In addition, large business corporations can generally offer their employees better insurance benefits, including workmen's compensation and increased retirement-fund withholding privileges.

An attorney can be helpful in incorporating. If you are concerned about tax planning or interested in obtaining corporate financing by selling shares to outsiders, you should obtain an experienced attorney and accountant versed in small-business planning: good professional advice can save you dollars and headaches in the long run. But if you are running a profitable sole proprietorship or partnership and are primarily interested in changing to the corporate form to limit your liability, you might well be able to suffer through the paperwork and incorporate yourself.

Follow certain steps when incorporating by yourself. First choose a name that you like for your business. Then call the agency that handles incorporations in your state (see Appendix III) to make sure that your business name has not already been taken. Include the designation "Incorporated," "Inc." "Company," or "Co." to indicate your business's status as a corporation. ("Limited" is the British term and can generally be used in this country only as part of a trade name.) The law usually requires that this form of notice be given to those doing business with a corporation as opposed to a sole proprietorship or a partnership.

Next, apply to the IRS for an employer identification number—you will not be able to open a corporate savings or checking account without it. The application for an employer identification number can take up to six weeks for IRS to process.

Then apply for your certificate of incorporation. Check Appendix III to find the agency in your state that handles incorporations and request that it send you model forms. You can also buy certificate-of-incorporation forms at most commercial stationers. Make sure that your purpose clause is worded broadly enough for you to conduct the affairs of the business. Send the agency the completed certificate of incorporation, together with a money order or cashier's check for the proper amount. Cash or personal checks are generally unacceptable. After you receive notification of approval from the state, order a set of corporate records and a corporate seal from a commercial stationer. It may take a couple of weeks, but they are required by law. The simplest corporate-record set is a looseleaf binder which contains stock certificates, a stock transfer ledger in which the shareholders' names and addresses are recorded, pages to which you attach the filing receipt and a copy of the certificate of incorporation, and sample minutes of meetings and bylaws so that you can just fill in the blanks. Every corporation must go through this paperwork; even if it is completely owned by you, you must issue the stock certificates to yourself, enter the issuance in the corporate record book, and place the certificates in a safe-deposit box.

You will probably want to set up both a savings and a checking bank account once you have an employer identification number and a corporate seal, although neither account is necessarily required by law. Meetings *are* generally required by law; they are advisable in any event, if for no other reason than to periodically verify the existence of the business.

Finally, on the day that you begin your corporation, transfer the capital, assets, and liabilities into your corporation. You can then begin your business (and bookkeeping) as a corporate entity.

If you are determined to incorporate and keep books without the advice of an attorney or accountant, you should study the book *Inc. Yourself: How to Profit by Setting Up Your Own Corporation* by Judith H. McQuown (Warner Books, 1981). It is full of practical information and contains examples of the forms and bookkeeping necessary to set up and maintain a corporation.

Remember to comply with related laws. To comply with laws relating to workmen's compensation and withholding taxes, contact the Internal Revenue Service. To comply with minimum-wage laws, contact your state's department of licensing and regulation or the Department of Labor, which regulates federal minimum-wage laws.

Your Day in Court

14

Small Claims

*They have no lawyers among them, for they
consider them as a sort of people whose profession it is to disguise matters and to wrest the
laws; and therefore they think it is better that
every man should plead his own cause, and
trust it to the judge, as in other places the client
trusts it to a counsellor.*

—Sir Thomas More, UTOPIA

The good have no need of an advocate.

—Plutarch, LIVES

SOME people are just plain unreasonable and refuse to make
amends if they've done something which is harmful to you,
your property, or your pocketbook. But even among reasonable people, disputes occur every day that are often over relatively small matters which can generally be resolved in small-
claims courts (sometimes called people's court or district court
—see Appendix IV), where lawyers are not only unnecessary
but frequently unwelcome.

Cases Handled by a Small-Claims Court

Many different kinds of cases are brought before a small-claims court. Compelling people to pay money agreed to in a contract (including separation agreements and promissory notes) and getting compensation for services performed are probably the most frequently brought suits. Others include suing a landlord for the return of a security deposit (or suing tenants for rent due and damages); seeking compensation for defective merchandise and any resulting damages; bringing an insurance company to court when it fails to pay for claims on homeowner's, medical, or automobile policies; suing someone who performed poor or unnecessary repair services; asking a court for property damage in automobile-accident cases; bringing an action against municipalities and their agencies; asking compensation for intentional damage done to you or your property; and trying to recover for missing goods that were entrusted to someone else.

Certain types of cases must be filed in other courts. In general you can't go to small-claims court when you want to obtain a divorce, an adoption, a division of property, or a court order injunction against illegal conduct. Some states have special courts which handle all landlord-tenant disputes. But if all you want are money damages to compensate for losses for which another person is legally responsible, small-claims court is the right place to go.

The maximum amount you can hope to win in small-claims court varies from state to state, and the jurisdictional limits are often revised (usually upwards) by legislatures. At the time of publication, the range was from $150 to $5,000. (See Appendix IV.) You should check with your local small-claims clerk as to the current jurisdictional limitations.

If the amount you wish to recover is in excess of the small-claims limit, you have two choices: you may sue for the maximum amount and forgo the excess amount of your claim, or you may sue for the full amount in a higher court where the jurisdictional limit is greater. But understand that the services of an attorney are practically mandatory when suing in a higher court; in many cases it might be wiser to sue for the maximum amount possible in the small-claims court and save the fee you would otherwise pay an attorney.

Note that courts will generally not let you "split claims" by dividing a lawsuit in order to avoid the jurisdictional limitation. "Forum shopping"—picking the court most likely to be favorable—is also frowned upon. States usually demand that the person being sued (the *defendant*) either reside or do business where the small-claims court is located, or that the events which gave rise to the suit occurred in that jurisdiction. (For venues, see Appendix IV.) The general rule is that you can always sue a defendant in the county where he resides or where he is maintaining a place of business, and in most states you can sue in the county where the injury or property loss occurred. (In many states you can also sue a defendant wherever he was *supposed* to have carried out an agreement with you.) The rules regarding where to sue a given defendant likewise vary from state to state. The best way to ascertain the local rules is to contact the clerk of your nearest small-claims court, describe whom you intend to sue and over what, and ask where you may file an action.

Not all small-claims courts are the same. There are variations from state to state, as well as within a particular state. But all have relatively informal procedures. Lawyers are usually permitted, but most small claimants represent themselves.

Use your judgment in deciding whether your complaint is serious enough. Virtually any grievance that can be resolved by money damages will be addressed by a small-claims court, but a judge will not take kindly to what he considers a frivolous complaint. Use your best judgment and common sense. If you feel your problem is genuine and treat it seriously, you're likely to get a fair hearing.

Sue promptly upon realizing that your grievance cannot be resolved out of court. Most states have a two-year statute of limitations for the kinds of claims appropriate to a small-claims court, but some involve an even shorter period of limitations. On the other hand, the statute is often longer for contract actions. If you fail to bring suit within the statutory period, the defendant can escape an otherwise valid claim for damages. Since the periods of statutory limitations vary from state to state and differ according to the type of claims you are asserting, you should always check with the small-claims court clerk as to the limitation that applies to your case.

Once your claim is filed, most states require that your suit be heard within thirty days. (This is in stark contrast with the normal civil case, which often takes years before the parties reach court.)

In some states a corporation cannot sue in a small-claims action. The theory is that if a business receives the advantages of being incorporated, including limited liability in certain matters, it should not be permitted to use the simplified procedure to collect small claims. On the other hand, corporations can be sued as defendants: once sued, they may be allowed to bring a counterclaim against the plaintiff (even if they ask for more than in the original suit), and in some places they can even seek more money than the small-claims limit.

There are several disadvantages to suing in a small-claims court. The major drawback is the jurisdictional limitation on the amount which you can recover. Also, in most jurisdictions, once you file a small claim you waive any right you may have had to a jury trial. Finally, appeals from the judge's decision in a small-claims case are somewhat restricted (and generally unsuccessful). Practically speaking, your only day in court is at the time of the original hearing.

How to File

It is not difficult to file a claim in small-claims court. Look up the number of your local small-claims court in the phone book. (If you get stuck, try dialing Information.) Tell the court clerk where both you and the defendant live or work, the amount for which you want to sue, when the events underlying the suit arose, and the general nature of your claim. Be polite and brief. Ask the clerk whether that particular small-claims court has jurisdiction over the claim you described.

If the court is appropriate, find where it is located and ask the clerk the hours and days you can file a claim, the cost, and whether the filing fee should be in cash or by check. Ask him if any documents are needed for the case you described, and which ones must be brought to the hearing. You will probably be told to bring any applicable contracts, letters, canceled checks, promissory notes, leases, accident reports, and any estimates of damage or repair you may have in your possession. (Make sure to keep copies if you give any original documents to the clerk.)

You must be able to supply certain information about your opponent. You must usually give the full legal name of the person or corporation that you are suing. Avoid initials. When suing a married woman, use her full name and not the name of her husband (i.e., "Mary Smith" rather than "Mrs. John Smith").

Most states require a person to sue a business under its proper legal name. (New York is more flexible, allowing a defendant to be sued under its legal name *or* under the name it uses to conduct business.) Finding out the correct legal name of a business might take some investigation, including a few phone calls to local and state governmental offices. Remember that the business name printed on a sign, a bill, or a letterhead is not necessarily the correct legal name of the entity you intend to sue. You might try phoning or visiting the municipal or county clerk's office in the area where the defendant does business, since corporations operating under an assumed name usually are required by law to file a certificate of their true identity. Likewise, if the business requires a license (many do), it usually must apply for one under its legal name: try contacting the appropriate licensing board. Another source of information is the state and local business-tax offices (where businesses must register and file their tax returns). Note also that all corporations doing business in a state usually must register their legal name with a special state office, generally the Secretary of State.

If the business is a sole proprietorship or partnership, you should bring suit against the names of the individuals "doing business as" the name of the business (i.e., Mary Smith and Jane Jones doing business as "Ms. Prints"). Suing under the name of either the individuals alone or of the business alone is not sufficient. If the business is a corporation, however, suit is brought under the name of the corporation only—not the individuals who own or run the business.

You must also determine the proper legal address of the person whom you are suing before you can complete the claim form so that you can send the required notice to the defendant. The address should be as complete as possible. (Include the zip code.)

Before visiting the small-claims clerk, assemble any relevant documents, as mentioned before. In addition, try to figure out what kind of case you have (e.g., breach of contract; landlord-tenant dispute; negligence; failure to pay under an insurance contract; intentional damage; defective merchandise, etc.), and prepare a very brief summary of why you believe the defendant owes you money. Bring with you the defendant's correct legal name and complete address. And don't forget the money to pay the filing fee.

Small-claims clerks are instructed to be helpful. Either you or the small-claims clerk will fill out a form which will include the classification of the type of suit, the proper legal names of all the parties and their full addresses, the amount of money being claimed, and a brief explanation of why you are owed money by the defendant.

After you sign and date the form, and pay the filing fee, the clerk will give you a receipt. This should include the name of the case, a docket or case number, and the date of the scheduled court appearance. Be sure to keep this document, since you may have to present it or refer to it when you appear in court.

If you want to check a clerk's advice, ask him for the book in which the law is contained. Finally, don't become offended if the clerk tells you that you don't have a valid claim or points out some weakness to your case. He knows how the system works and is simply attempting to be helpful by keeping you from wasting your time. Sometimes they underestimate the strength of a claimant's case.

It doesn't cost much to sue in a small-claims court. Filing fees vary from state to state, but they generally range from two to ten dollars, plus the cost of serving notice upon the person against whom a claim is brought. If the court finds in your favor, you may recover these costs (as well as your damages) from the losing party.

The court notifies your opponent that he's being sued. After you file your claim with the clerk, a notice will be sent to the defendant telling him that he is being sued, the amount of damage being claimed, and the date and place of the trial. He will be notified by one of three methods: (a) personal service by a sheriff, marshal, or other authorized person (which can cost as much as $20.00; (b) registered mail with return receipt (the most common method); or (c) first-class mail. Registered mail with return receipt is preferred over first-class mail since it assures proof of receipt of the notice by the defendant. Even if he refuses to pick up his registered mail at the post office, the process is still considered by most courts to be sufficient service—so that if he doesn't show up, the judge will hear your case and can enter a judgment in your favor.

Beware of "sovereign immunity." *Sovereign immunity* applies principally to the state and federal government. It is usually necessary to consult with an attorney before suing either a federal or state agency. On the other hand, your local government is often subject to the same kinds of claims as are individuals and corporations. An exception is a negligence action, for which a notice-of-claim form must be filed with the government before you can sue. It should be available from officials at the government agency office you wish to sue.

The usual time period in which the claim must be filed is from sixty to ninety days between the event which led to your suit and your filing a notice of claim, but it can vary from three days in some jurisdictions to 120 in others. If you don't file the notice, you can't file a lawsuit.

The purpose of a claim notice is to allow the municipal body to investigate the validity of your claim before a lawsuit is begun. The notice of claim must usually be sworn to in front of a notary public. It states your name, address, the time and place of the event in question, and the damages you have suffered. Usually, it can be personally served upon a designated agent for the governmental body, or sent by registered or certified mail.

If you are filing a claim against a town, you may generally serve the town clerk; if against a city, the city clerk; if against the local school district, you generally have your choice of serving any member of the school board or the secretary of the board. Don't be shy about asking questions; governments today are so used to being sued they are no longer insulted by such questions.

You do not have to wait for the bureaucracy to act on your claim. Even if the public official has assured you that your claim will be paid, the statute of limitations may begin to run from the moment the event which is the focus of the suit actually occurred. Unless there is a mandatory waiting period, once you have filed a notice of claim as required, you can proceed directly to the small-claims court. Bring proof with you that you have already forwarded a notice of claim to the local governmental body (have the person receiving it sign on your copy). Then file your claim with the small-claims clerk just as you would if it were an ordinary case.

If you are injured by someone who is employed by someone else, sue both. If the person who causes your injury did so while acting as an employee of someone else, you should sue *both* the employee and his employer. Under the legal doctrine of *respondeat superior* (Latin for "let the master answer"), an employer is ordinarily liable for legal wrongs committed by his employees within the scope of their employment. But you should sue the employee as well, in case the judge finds that the employee was *not* acting within the scope of his employment when the injury occurred. Of course, you will be allowed only one recovery of damages.

There are different ways to determine how much to sue for. The law has developed different ways by which damages can be measured, depending on the facts involved. In a breach-of-contract case, for example, you are entitled to be "made whole again"—that is, to be put in as good a position as you would have occupied if the defendant had performed his obligations rather than breaching his contract with you. The person suing must be prepared to show that he made reasonable efforts to keep his losses at a minimum (like trying to re-rent an apartment that has been vacated).

In cases involving property damages resulting from the intentional or negligent acts of another, the general measure of damages is this: the fair market value of your property just before the accident, or the amount of money it would take to restore it to the condition it was in just before the incident occurred—whichever sum is lower.

The measure of damages in a personal injury case (where

you are hurt as a result of either the intentional or the negligent acts of another) is less cut and dried. Assuming you can prove that the person being sued is legally responsible for your injuries, you may claim damages for present and future medical bills and lost wages; pain and suffering; mental distress; and, in a defamation case, the injury to your reputation. Putting a dollar value on the latter items is often subjective, and if you were severely hurt, your recovery is likely to be in excess of the small-claims limit.

Finally, in some consumer protection cases, you may be allowed by law to collect statutory penalties: amounts of money over and above your true losses. But this is the only time a plaintiff might expect to wind up in a better position than had he not been injured.

The general rule is that you cannot recover punitive damages—designed to "teach a lesson" to the guilty party—in a small-claims action.

Separation Agreements

You can use a small-claims action to enforce a separation agreement. The key to bringing an action in a small-claims court on a separation agreement is not to let the overdue amount exceed the limits of jurisdiction for that court. You should consider a small-claims court action, therefore, even when your spouse is only a few weeks late in making the agreed-upon payments.

Note that if there was no separation agreement—that is, if the terms of a divorce decree were resolved by a judge at trial —they may be enforced only by the court that awarded the decree. A small-claims court can enforce the terms of an agreement or a contract, but not an order of a higher court. (See Chapter 6 for information about court-awarded decrees.)

You should copy the appropriate section of the agreement, highlight the clause specifying payment, and bring it to court. Also bring a copy of the entire original agreement in case the judge wishes to examine the signatures. In addition, prepare a list of payments made and their dates (typed, if possible), together with an indication of the payments missed. Try to handle the matter as a simple breach-of-contract case, avoiding all discussion of the misbehavior and character flaws of your spouse that led to the breakup of the marriage. The small-claims judge is likely to be grateful to any party taking "the high road" in a domestic-relations matter.

Settlements

Don't file a small claim before trying to work out a settlement with your opponent. On the other hand, one should always be wary of the defendant who tries to avoid liability by pretending to be engaged in good-faith negotiations while in fact trying to divert the potential plaintiff from filing his claim until after the statutory limitations period has run out. Despite this caution, it is always wise to precede the filing of an actual small-claims suit with a well-thought-out, neatly typed settlement letter sent to your adversary.

The letter should be civil, polite, and to the point—not sarcastic or antagonistic. It should state your grievance (i.e., the factual situation and the monetary losses you have suffered), demand compensation, and say that you are prepared to sue for damages if you don't receive satisfaction within a specified time. The letter may intimidate its recipient to the point of negotiation, but even if it doesn't, it serves two other important functions. First, it satisfies the requirement of some states that a person make a demand upon his adversary for payment prior to filing a small-claims case against him. Second, the letter will be useful as evidence in the small-claims court, where it should serve as a summary of your case to which the judge can refer when he or she is tying together the pieces of your claim. An appropriate deadline for response is generally two weeks. Keep at least two exact copies of the letter you sent—one for use in court and one for your personal file.

Send the letter by registered mail, return receipt requested. This method will provide you a post-office slip to offer as evidence to the court that you made a mailing to your adversary on a specific date, as well as the further evidence of a return postcard to prove your opponent received the envelope.

Once your suit is filed in the small-claims court, keep in mind that a settlement is still possible. If the logic of your settlement letter or the actual notice that he is being sued belatedly puts your adversary into a negotiating mood, it shouldn't hurt to discuss matters with him. Explain your position anticipating an offer of settlement. If your opponent merely rants and raves, interrupt him calmly with the suggestion that he call you back when he has regained his composure.

The general (though not necessarily best) advice is to reject initial settlement offers, and to make a stiff counteroffer instead. It is a good technique to assure your adversary you'll give serious consideration to whatever he decides is his best offer. And it is a vital rule to be sure to put any offer which is made and accepted into writing, signed by both parties. *Never* settle for an oral agreement. Once a written agreement is signed, you have a binding contract which itself can be enforced in court should your adversary later try to renege on any part of his obligations.

If you are able to settle the dispute prior to trial, you should notify the court clerk that neither you nor your opponent will be appearing before the court on the day scheduled for your trial.

If you decide to accept your opponent's offer on the day of trial, you should both appear before the judge when your case is called. Inform the court clerk or the judge that a settlement has been reached. Request the judge to enter judgment in your favor for the amount that was agreed upon. If the defendant is prepared to pay you right there in court, the judge can dismiss your case. The advantage to both parties appearing in court and reporting the settlement to the judge is that if either of you later reneges, the matter may be either rescheduled without filing a new claim, or an automatic judgment may be granted against the party not adhering to the settlement.

Preparing for Your Day in Court

Know your case. By the time you have talked with the small-claims clerk and filled out your claims form, you should be aware of the important elements of your case. That is, you should already have a good idea of the facts you will be expected to prove to persuade the judge to rule in your favor.

The next step is to organize the relevant documents and ask any witness who you feel is important to come to court on the day of your trial. Remember that the number of witnesses does nothing to enhance your claim. The judge will be influenced only by those witnesses who actually observed or know something relevant to your case.

If you believe that physical or demonstrative evidence will simplify or clarify your claim, prepare appropriate charts or diagrams. In cases involving defective merchandise or similar physical evidence, bring the articles into the courtroom whenever possible. Otherwise, photographs showing what you are trying to describe are usually helpful: pictures that need an extensive explanation, however, are often worthless.

You might want to visit the small-claims court before your trial date to become familiar with the procedures and general atmosphere of "rough justice" in the "people's court."

In some jurisdictions, you can present statements of witnesses without asking them to appear personally in court. Check with the clerk to see if a statement would be satisfactory. Certain written statements, such as those concerning repair estimates, are usually permitted. Most often, though, courts will not accept testimony from an absent witness (the so-called "hearsay" evidence) because he or she cannot be cross-examined by the other party.

If you want a particular witness in court and that person will not appear voluntarily, you may ask the clerk to issue a *subpoena* (a court order requiring a witness to appear at the time a case is heard). State laws vary, but you may have to arrange to have the subpoena properly served and pay certain mileage costs and a witness fee to the person you subpoena. Perhaps the most important consideration before requesting the issuance of a subpoena, however, is to question whether the testimony of a witness who has been dragged into the courtroom against his will is really going to be helpful in your case.

If you require a document or records (particularly from your opponent), you may ask the clerk to issue a *subpoena duces tecum.* This document will require that the person who has custody of the records or documents deliver the items to the court before you present your case.

Be patient. It generally takes about a month between filing and a court date, but this waiting period can vary from two weeks to four months.

What to Do and Say in Court

Look forward to informality. Arrive early, dressed in something neat, presentable, and comfortable. Expect to see many other people waiting to have their claims heard. In addition, there will usually be a stenographer, clerk, and court attendant in the courtroom. The stenographer records everything that is said on the record; a number of courts now use tape recorders. The court clerk is there to assist you and the judge in handling the evidence and making the proper entries into court files. The attendant acts something like an usher and keeps order in the courtroom.

After you are seated, the judge will enter and the clerk or bailiff will say something like, "All rise!" Everyone stands for a moment, until the judge himself is seated. The docket of cases is then called to determine which parties are present. (Many plaintiffs and defendants fail to appear.) When your name is called, you should answer, "Ready." When the clerk calls your case, walk up to the railing (with your witnesses, if any). The clerk will swear you in by administering an oath, and the trial will begin.

Your opponent may not appear. If your opponent has failed to appear after having been properly served, the judge will ask you to establish a *prima facie* case. This means that you have to give the judge enough evidence proving your case that he will be justified in granting an award. If damages are legally recoverable, you will be awarded a default judgment. The judgment should also include the court costs you have paid (and, occasionally, legal interest). Once you are granted a default judgment, contact the clerk for advice on how to collect the judgment.

If the reason your opponent failed to appear was that he was never served a summons, you will have to come back on another court date after the respondent is properly served. (Many debtors are experts at avoiding service.) Make arrangements with the clerk for another attempt at serving notice.

The claimant speaks first. If the defendant answers, "Ready," when your case is called, you will be asked by the judge to present your claim first. Try to be calm, brief, and courteous. Outline to the court what your claim is about, how it arose and why you believe your opponent owes you a specific sum of money. Offer your settlement letter into evidence, along with the original of any other documents or physical evidence you have prepared. If you have any estimates, bills, letters, or other documents for the court to view, make sure to have copies for yourself and your opponent. You may ask your witnesses, if any, to testify on your behalf. If the judge asks any questions, answer them as directly as possible, addressing him as "Your Honor."

Try to anticipate your opponent's case.

For example, even if a defendant would otherwise be held legally responsible for your loss, he can avoid liability if he can show that the statute of limitations has run out on your claim (that is, you've waited too long to assert your grievance), or that you signed a release or waiver allowing him to act as he did. Thus it is wise to scrutinize even the most meritorious case for fatal flaws such as these before going through the effort to initiate a small-claims suit.

Your opponent will then be given the opportunity to respond. You should let him speak without interruption. Generally, the time for asking questions is after your opponent has completed his presentation. The best rule is to look to the judge for direction in this matter, since each judge conducts the hearing differently.

The importance of being polite to the judge and to your opponent cannot be overemphasized. Failing to be courteous harms your case by distracting the judge, and impairing your effectiveness and credibility. It is also important to avoid trying to act like a lawyer during a small-claims court proceeding; using legalese will probably backfire. Finally, don't overextend your welcome: expect your presentation to be completed in less than fifteen minutes. If you are still talking and the judge asks you to wrap up, do so quickly for maximum effectiveness.

The hearing will not last long. Usually a small-claims hearing will not take longer than twenty minutes. After the judge has heard both sides, he may render a decision immediately and attempt to work out a payment schedule. Or he may decide to reserve judgment—to think about the facts or to research the law. If this happens, you will generally be notified of the result within a few days.

Collecting Judgments

The defendant may not pay immediately. After you receive word of the judgment, you should contact the losing party, preferably by mail, and ask for payment within ten days. (This should not be his first notification, since he was informed of the decision by the court at the same time you were.) If he chooses to pay the sum of the judgment directly to the court, the clerk will accept a check and place it in the court account; you will be paid once the check has cleared. If the defendant pays the judgment directly to you, you should advise the clerk of that fact.

If your adversary does not pay the amount awarded voluntarily, you will have to avail yourself of the local remedies associated with your status as that of a *judgment creditor*.

You may have to do some detective work to find out the nature and location of the defendant's assets before returning to the small-claims court to obtain a court order known as a *writ of execution*. If possible, discover where he works, banks, runs a business, or owns real estate or personal property (cars, boats, expensive stereo systems, etc.). Note that, in general, any property owned by both a defendant and his wife as tenants by the entirety is *judgment-proof* if your judgment is against him alone. (Practically speaking, any jointly owned property is difficult to seize. Sheriffs most often go after wages and bank accounts.) Once you ascertain the defendant's assets, return to the small-claims court. The clerk will send you to the civil enforcement officer who deals with civil awards and court orders, usually called a sheriff, marshal, or constable. Tell him what you've discovered about the defendant's assets. The officer will obtain from the clerk a document called an *execution of judgment* and attempt to notify the respondent that he must pay the judgment. If the payment is still not forthcoming, the officer may seize assets, tie up bank accounts, *attach* personal property, or *garnish* the wages of the respondent. Generally up to 10 percent of the gross wages earned may be subject to garnishment. If the respondent is self-employed, the court may issue an *installment-payment order* for a certain amount to be paid each week to the court officer.

If the respondent has real property such as land, a home, or a building, you should file the judgment in the county clerk's office or with the property registrar in the locale of the property. The judgment will then serve as a lien against the real property—that is, the property cannot be transferred to a new owner until the judgment is paid in full. If a judgment is not paid promptly, interest from the date of the award to the time of payment is added.

Collection procedures differ from state to state. Once you have made friends with the small-claims court clerk, the procedure won't seem as intimidating. Certain states are more helpful than others in small-claims matters.

New Yorkers, for example, are given by law some special legal ammunition for collecting judgments from slow-paying businesses. The business must pay the judgment within thirty-five days after being notified by the court. If the thirty-five-day deadline passes, the plaintiff will be entitled to sue the business all over again—but this time the amount of damages will be for the amount of the original unpaid judgment *plus* reasonable attorney's fees *plus* a statutory penalty of $100. New York law also provides for treble damage awards (three times actual damages) against businesses that have not paid at least three small-claims court judgments.

Besides notifying the clerk of the small-claims court of payment, you should also inform any other place where you have filed a judgment that the amount has been paid in full. This is called filing a satisfaction. Your failure to do so may unjustifiably affect the defendant's credit record. In some states, failure to file a satisfaction is a violation of the law.

15

Traffic Violations

. . . back to thy punishment,
False fugitive, and to thy speed add wings.
—Milton, PARADISE LOST

For most Americans, contesting a ticket in Traffic Court not only is their first contact with the judicial system but frequently is the most frustrating. Nevertheless, time-consuming and troublesome as it may be, thousands of people across the country appear for their day in court. Only a fraction are represented by lawyers; the rest fend, with similar results, for themselves.

If you get a ticket and decide it's worth the time, money, and frustration to fight it, there are a few things worth knowing. The first is that, with or without a lawyer, very few people win when it's their word against the cop's. Where you've been "caught by radar," your chances of success are even more slight, and even the best lawyer will find his hands tied. So, generally speaking, unless the offense is one for which a serious punishment is involved (such as jail or loss of your driver's license), or there is an injury to someone else or damage to property, representing yourself is probably a good idea.

Whatever you do, there are a number of steps to take that will make your life much easier later on.

At the Time of the Incident

Cooperate as fully as possible when you're stopped by a traffic officer. The law dictates that you show him your driver's license and registration. Common sense dictates that you should show him courtesy. If he's annoyed by your attitude, he's more likely to look for additional violations (such as equipment failures). If you remain pleasant, there's always a chance he'll give you a break. Once he starts writing your name, however, you can be certain you'll get either a warning or a ticket.

Answer any identification questions politely. Take your driver's license out of your wallet yourself and hand it to the officer. (Giving the whole wallet to the officer is a gesture traditionally associated with the offering of a bribe.) Ask the officer if you can look in the glove compartment for your registration—lunging for the glove compartment could alarm him, and most officers will appreciate the request. If the officer doesn't tell you immediately, ask why you were stopped and listen carefully to the answer. Ask him how you were caught. If what he says at the time of the violation differs from his story at trial, it will weaken his case in court. If he says you were caught by radar, ask to see his tuning fork. If he is unable to show you one, it casts more than a little doubt as to whether he had calibrated the unit before and after your alleged violation. Finally—unless you really were rushing your pregnant wife to the hospital to have a baby—fight the impulse to play "true confessions." An admission of guilt is almost certain to be written down in the officer's notes and can be used against you in court.

Sign the citation even if you don't think you're guilty. Signing a citation is not an admission of guilt—only a promise to appear in court at the time and date specified. On the other hand, if you refuse to sign the citation, the officer generally has no choice but to arrest you and escort you into jail until a judge can hear your case.

Gather the facts. Make notes of what happened: when and where you were at the time, your speed, the weather, traffic conditions, etc. This data will be useful should you decide to plead Not Guilty and stand trial. In addition, you may want to draw a diagram of the scene and take photographs.

Finally, if there is a space on the citation where you can request the presence of the officer at the time of trial, check it off. You may want to cross-examine him. Moreover, if he fails to appear, the case may be dismissed.

Do the same things if you get a traffic ticket while out-of-state. The procedure to be followed is often the same: After you sign the citation, you make the choice between traveling out-of-state again to defend yourself in court or simply paying the bail (in effect, the fine) when you receive the ticket, and then forfeiting it by not showing up in court. The latter choice has the same effect as if you had pleaded guilty and paid a fine. In some tourist-oriented cities, the general policy is to avoid giving tickets to out-of-state motorists, on the grounds that forcing them to appear on a later date would be unfair. But in some areas, the officer may ask a tourist to follow him to the nearest judge so that the case can be heard immediately. You may have to post bond to ensure your return; a failure to appear could result in an automatic plea of guilty and a forfeiture of your bond as the fine.

An officer can confiscate your license in some instances. If any part of the license has been altered, if the license has somebody else's name or picture on it, or if you have more than one license, it may be taken away from you. Sometimes, if the trial is scheduled for a distant court, the officer will take your license to ensure that you will appear to reclaim it. This acts much the same as an appearance bond. At the scene of an accident, an officer will often take the licenses of drivers, passengers, and witnesses to make sure that they all stay around until he has finished his report and recorded their statements.

Tickets and Warnings

There is a difference between a warning and a ticket. A warning will often be titled "Notice of Vehicle Code Violation" or "Traffic Warning," and can be given for parking, defective equipment, or moving violations. Parking and moving warnings usually require no independent action on your part. Equipment warnings require you to have the violations corrected and certified within a given period of time, usually fifteen days; they often have a provision for mailing in an attached form after the violation has been corrected. (Be sure to do so, or you may get a ticket for failing to correct your equipment violation in time.)

A ticket or citation is actually a written promise by you to appear in court for an alleged violation on a specific date and time. Technically, your ticket represents an arrest; the officer is releasing you from his custody on your promise that you will face the charges.

If there is nothing else suspicious and you look like an honest citizen, many officers will let you off with a warning. Even if the officer does give you a citation for not having a license or registration card, most courts will dismiss the case if you can present a license or registration in court that was valid at the time of your violation.

"Moving violations" involving the use of alcohol are the most serious. The most common types of tickets received by today's motorists are those for moving violations; equipment, parking, pedestrian, and citations for not having a license or registration card; and tickets in which the use of alcohol is involved—for which the penalties are usually the most severe.

Moving violations cover a variety of offenses, such as exceeding the local basic speed law or the posted maximum limit;

violating rights-of-way; failing to obey a traffic-signal light or stop sign; and performing various types of illegal turns.

A person violates the basic speed law by driving faster than is safe in areas where no limits are posted—or where weather or road conditions make a slower speed than that posted advisable. Thus a motorist can receive a ticket for doing 30 mph in a heavy rain while traveling through a zone posted at 45 mph.

A driver who exceeds the speed limit actually posted on a roadway has committed a *prima facie* speed violation—that is, he is *presumed* to have been driving at an unreasonable and improper speed, and will be found guilty unless he can prove that this speed was not unsafe when the condition of the highway (traffic congestion, visibility, and the like) is considered. But if a person is charged with violating the state's *maximum* speed limit (currently, 55 mph in all states), the circumstances will have no bearing whatsoever. Unless he can prove the charging officer was in error, or establish a reasonable doubt that the charging officer made a mistake, he'll be found guilty.

Violations involving rights-of-way occur when a person fails to yield to emergency vehicles, to cars already in an intersection, to horses in an equestrian crossing, or to pedestrians in a crosswalk. One is also required to yield the right-of-way to other vehicles when making a left turn, when making a right turn on a red signal (where permitted by state law), when approaching a "Yield" sign, when turning onto a public road from a driveway or other private road, and when entering traffic from an alley. Generally, any time your actions on a highway interfere with another vehicle's use of that highway, and you cause them to brake, swerve, or otherwise avoid your vehicle, you have violated their right-of-way.

Parking violations are the most common. A parking violation occurs any time a vehicle is parked in an illegal place or manner, or at an illegal time. The ticket is issued to the owner of the vehicle, and is written, filed, processed, and recorded by reference to your license plate rather than your driver's license.

Most states hold the registered owner of the vehicle responsible if it was illegally parked, regardless of who was driving. The only way to establish someone else's responsibility is to prove that the vehicle was stolen, or that it had been loaned, rented, leased, or sold to someone else at the time of the violation.

You may automatically get a ticket if you're involved in an accident. An accident citation is a ticket written by a traffic officer and issued to a driver who caused an accident, or to any driver involved in one. It is not based on the officer's actual observation of the accident, but upon the officer's assessment of the evidence collected at the scene after an accident has occurred: statements from witnesses and drivers, skid marks, and the like. The ticket may be presented at the time of the accident, or it may be mailed to you a few days later.

Attorneys

Accident citations usually require a lawyer's attention. Defending oneself against an accident citation is very important. A guilty verdict will often be admitted into evidence in a civil suit arising from the accident, and a great deal of money could be involved. This is one time when you should seriously consider having an attorney for a traffic court offense.

You should also hire the best attorney you can find if you are charged with a serious moving offense, such as automobile manslaughter, driving under a suspended license, recklessness due to alcohol. These are jailable offenses, and you might have the right to be represented by a public defender if you cannot afford to hire a lawyer. If you have a poor driving record and are in danger of losing your license, hiring an attorney is a good idea. Make sure, however, that the attorney you hire is familiar with (and effective in) traffic court matters. Like doctors, attorneys are specialists. Unless he or she has expertise in traffic court or "driving under the influence" defense work, you probably won't be getting your money's worth.

You can usually get the violation explained to you. Obviously, you must understand your violation before you can decide how to prepare a defense. You can try phoning the agency which issued the citation, but the knowledge and solicitude of the person who takes your call will vary greatly. If you aren't satisfied with his response, his agency's Public Information Officer may be more helpful (see Appendix V). Try to get a definition of your violation which you can break down into separate elements. Unless you believe that the state can prove beyond a reasonable doubt that each of the separate elements was present at the time of the alleged violation, you should consider pleading Not Guilty.

Arraignment and Pleas

Read the dockets first. Find and read the court dockets (lists of cases to be heard) to determine the room where your case will be heard. These are usually computer printouts containing your name, citation number, and courtroom and are posted prominently. Then go the appropriate courtroom and notify the clerk or bailiff that you are present. He'll probably tell you to have a seat until your case is called. When that happens you will have the opportunity to make your plea to a judge. This is known as an arraignment. The judge will call your name, read off the charge against you, and ask how you plead.

Know the kinds of pleas that are available. The usual choice of pleas is from among the following: Guilty, Guilty with an Explanation, Not Guilty, and *Nolo Contendere* (or No Contest). If you plead "Not Guilty," a trial will ensue.

When in doubt, plead Not Guilty. If you have any doubts as to your guilt, by all means plead Not Guilty. The worst that can happen will be that the judge will find you Guilty and probably assess the same penalty as if you had admitted your guilt or not appeared in court. Many attorneys would advise that, if you take the time and trouble to go to court in the first place, a Not Guilty plea will accomplish the same purpose as a Guilty with an Explanation plea—a reduced fine or fewer points on your record. Conversely, a bare plea of Guilty is usually a waste of time—in most cases you could have done the same by mail.

If you decide to plead Guilty, you can sometimes skip the arraignment and send the court (before the hearing) what is technically the bail money—the amount specified on the citation or on a notice sent to you in the mail. (You may have to appear if you were charged with driving while intoxicated.) If you mail in the bail and then fail to appear in court, the money is forfeited at the time of your trial. The offense is recorded on your driver's record the same as if you had pleaded Guilty and paid a fine.

If you want to plead Not Guilty but can't appear in person at the specified time or arraignment, you can usually plead Not Guilty by mail or by appearing in court prior to the hearing date. A final, more expensive, option is to appear by proxy— that is, to have an attorney appear at the arraignment and plead on your behalf.

Don't fail to appear at the arraignment or neglect to send in bail. You must appear—unless you are prepared for a lot of trouble (such as having your license renewal held up, and even the possibility of imprisonment).

"Guilty with an Explanation" means Guilty. For purposes of your record, the two pleas are the same. If you plead Guilty with an Explanation, you are hoping that court will suspend or reduce the amount of fine (and, in some states, the number of points).

Your explanation should be concise, to the point, and offered in a respectful manner. Don't deny that you committed the violation after making this plea, because the judge will probably either tell you to plead Not Guilty, or become irritated and cut you off short and sentence you. Simply outline the factors you believe should mitigate your punishment: good prior driving record, bad weather conditions, light traffic, etc. Try to maintain an attitude of polite contrition. Avoid groveling.

Nolo Contendere **affords small protection.** Again, as far as your driving record is concerned, a plea of *Nolo Contendere* is the same as a guilty plea. However, in a subsequent civil suit against you resulting from an accident in which you received a citation, the plea of *Nolo Contendere* cannot generally be used against you as an admission of guilt.

The judge can't look at your record before the trial if you plead Not Guilty. Sometimes the judge will simply ask you about your driving record, and sometimes he will look it up. Most courts nowadays have computerized retrieval systems. The judge often bases his sentence on your record. Good drivers may be put on probation, without even a fine. Repeat offenders may be fined the maximum allowed by law or have their licenses suspended or revoked.

Note, however, that if you plead Not Guilty and proceed to trial, it is improper for the judge to consider your past record in deciding guilt or innocence. (The theory is that you are being tried for this one incident, and not for a propensity to commit a certain type of offense; admitting as evidence your prior similar convictions is considered prejudicial.) But the judge can (and often does) refer to past records when passing sentence.

You can ask for a continuance (postponement). Following your arraignment, if you have pleaded Not Guilty you have a constitutional right to a speedy trial. On the other hand, if you need more time to consider the charges against you, to construct a defense, or to hire an attorney, you can (and should) ask for a continuance. The prosecutor may also ask for a continuance, but unless you too have asked for one (thereby waiving your right to a quick trial), the prosecutor cannot be granted a continuance beyond the period within which you are guaranteed a speedy trial (generally a month to a month and a half after the arraignment). Prosecutors are not generally granted continuances when the officer involved does not appear for the trial; instead, the judge may dismiss the case. This is particularly true in states where the officer serves as the prosecutor.

Quite often a continuance can be to your strategic advantage. By extending the period of time between your violation and the actual trial, you increase the chances of the officer's not being available, his memory of the incident fading, and the evidence being lost or misplaced. The prosecutor generally needs the police officer's personal testimony in order to present his case.

Do not agree to a trial by deposition. A trial by deposition is one where the evidence against you is an officer's own out-of-court statement of the facts, generally his written investigative report. Do not agree to such a trial, because you cannot cross-examine (question) a piece of paper. As the defendant, you have the constitutional right to be confronted by your accuser.

Trial

Prepare well. Preparation of a defense should really begin the moment you are stopped by the officer. Avoid making any statements which you wouldn't want to hear again at the trial. Obtain names of witnesses. Draw a diagram of the scene; take photographs if you feel they'll be useful. As soon as possible, make notes to yourself of what happened: write down everything you remember the officer saying to you; when and where you were at the time of the incident; the speed of your car and the others around you; the weather, lighting, and traffic conditions. Remember, all of this is essential even if you eventually hire a lawyer.

Next you should check the elements of the violation in your state's Vehicle Code. Decide whether you want any witnesses to testify, and whether any physical evidence, such as photographs or drawings, could strengthen your case. You can subpoena witnesses or physical evidence not in your possession, if you believe such evidence is necessary to your case. Finally, prepare your own testimony, as well as questions you want to ask the police officer and any other witnesses you expect the prosecution to use.

Don't rely on the officer's diagram and photographs. Chances are he won't have any. If he does, there is no legal reason you can't use his evidence—but there are good reasons for relying upon your own. If your diagram conflicts with the officer's, and your diagram is found to be correct, the officer's credibility will be damaged.

If your case centers upon your visual perception of the area, photographs can be important to your defense—and it is doubtful the officer will provide any. For example, photographs showing a stop sign blocked by a tree, or the sun setting majestically behind a traffic light, could vividly illustrate your testimony that you never saw the light at all, let alone that it was red.

Most traffic-court cases are finished in a few minutes. Depending on the jurisdiction, you are usually scheduled to appear in the courtroom in either the morning or the afternoon. Expect to spend the greater part of a half day in traffic court: your case will probably be one of many, and it may be hours before your name is called. Generally all violations written by a particular traffic officer are scheduled together.

This may be convenient for the officer, but not for you. You can make the best of it by using this opportunity to observe how the judge handles similar cases—to which defenses he's sympathetic, how he treats speeders, the effects on his decision of a good driving record, etc.

Divide the violation charge into manageable parts. You should make sure the prosecution produces evidence that each of the elements needed for conviction was present at the time of your alleged violation. If only one element is missing, you technically have not committed the violation and should be found Not Guilty. It's more likely that the evidence to support one or more of the elements will be weak. In that case you should emphasize this weakness by cross-examination or with your own contradictory evidence. The important thing to remember is that the state has the burden of proving you were guilty beyond a reasonable doubt. You don't have to prove you are innocent in order to win.

Don't talk until the judge tells you to. The state's (prosecution's) argument is presented first, usually through testimony by a police officer.

Ask relevant questions. All of your questions should be oriented toward the goal of establishing a reasonable doubt of the officer's observation of your violation. In most traffic cases, the state's case against you is made up primarily of the testimony of the police officer. If you can prove that the officer was mistaken at the time of the offense, or that the equipment he used could have been malfunctioning, or that his story at the time of the trial is different from what he told you at the time of the offense, you have created sufficient doubt of your guilt that the judge should dismiss the case. In addition, if you can prove that the officer did not establish the existence of all the elements of your violation, your case should be dismissed by the judge as a matter of law.

During cross-examination you might ask the police officer about his location at the time he first observed your vehicle; what he was doing at the time; the conditions (weather and traffic) under which he observed you; his observation and memory of the location of the offense; and his observation of your alleged violation. Listen carefully for any discrepancies, inaccuracies, or contradictions in his answers (take notes if you can). If he testifies that he clocked your vehicle with his speedometer, make him prove that it was a calibrated speedometer; ask when it was calibrated, who did the work, and what their qualifications were for the job.

Above all, maintain a polite and respectful demeanor. Your best bet for winning will be to prove that this very human traffic officer made a simple mistake in your case. Being openly suspicious and resentful toward the officer will only make him a more sympathetic witness. Remember that most courts nurture the myth that the officer is a neutral witness with no ax to grind. Moreover, most judges—whether they admit it or not—tend to presume the validity of the state's case over yours.

Ask to see the officer's notes. Since the officer is probably basing his testimony almost entirely on his notes, you should definitely ask to see them. If the favorable information outweighs the unfavorable information, ask the judge to enter the notes into evidence. If the officer testifies to anything during the trial that is not written on the citation or in his notes, you should challenge that portion of his testimony: point out that he has written many tickets in addition to yours and there is a good chance he could have been mistaken about the facts, and that your memory of the event and your own notes are at least as good as his recollection.

Make your argument after the state rests its case. After the prosecution has presented its evidence, you have cross-examined the opposing witnesses, and the state has rested its case, make your argument. If you can make any argument that the prosecution did not establish all the elements of its violation beyond a reasonable doubt, make it then and ask the judge to dismiss the case against you. If he grants your motion, the case ends in your favor.

If the judge denies your motion to dismiss, the next step is to present your defense. This should include your own testimony and that of witnesses, any physical evidence (such as photographs), and a closing argument. Your testimony and closing argument should be concise, well organized, and prepared in advance. An outline of the points you want to cover is often helpful. Do not read, since you shouldn't lose the chance to have direct eye contact with the judge.

Be calm when being cross-examined. If you or any witness testifies in court, you must give the opposing side the opportunity of cross-examination. The best advice is to think before you speak, hold your temper, and refrain from arguing. Do your best to answer the questions; try not to take personally the state's attitude that you are obviously lying or contradicting yourself. (It's all part of the game the prosecutor learned in law school.)

Radar Cases

Winning a radar case is difficult. In many states your chances range from slim to none. A recent study in Maryland concluded that the overwhelming majority (up to 96 percent) of those charged with a speeding violation that had been detected by radar were found guilty. However, some jurisdictions —Florida in particular—have thrown out thousands of radar cases on the grounds of equipment unreliability. You might try asking a lawyer friend about chances of winning a radar case in your state. If he indicates the judges have open minds— which, though a Constitutional requirement, is unlikely in radar cases—by all means try to fight the alleged violation.

Although many court observers feel that the chances of winning a radar case are minimal because most judges continue to be swayed by the "objective" proof of guilt provided by machinery, if you really want to fight a radar-generated speeding ticket you should study *The Ticket Book*, by Rod Dornsife (a former traffic officer).

If your citation involved the use of radar and your state law requires a Traffic Engineering Survey, be sure to check with the engineering department of your city or county to see if a valid survey exists. If your state, county, or local laws require that radar warning signs be posted, make sure that the signs were posted correctly in compliance with the law.

The prosecution must establish its case. The prosecution, through its witness, the police officer, has to establish the time, place, and location of the offense, and show that you were the driver of the offending vehicle. He must prove that the state laws regarding speed limits and radar signs were complied with, and that your speed was "unreasonable" or in excess of the 55 mph maximum limit. He must give his qualifications and training in radar operation, and testify that the unit was operating correctly and had been tested for accuracy. Finally, he must be able to identify your vehicle and testify that it was out in front, by itself, and nearest the radar unit when the reading was obtained. Keep in mind that radar is only a tool used to verify the officer's visual observation, which must be stated. All these elements have to be established by the state beyond a reasonable doubt.

In a radar case you should ask the same questions regarding the calibrating of the unit by a radar tuning fork as you would ask about a calibrated speedometer. If you had asked to see the tuning fork at the time of the incident and been refused, be sure to bring that out at trial. Ask specifically if the officer calibrates his unit with a fork at the beginning and end of every shift, and before and after every violation. If he replies no, ask him whether he is aware of the manufacturer's recommendation that the radar operator calibrate his unit at those times.

Sentences

The judge decides quickly. The judge usually decides and delivers the verdict immediately after the case has been heard. If he finds you Not Guilty, the citation will not appear on your permanent driving record, and you are entitled to a full refund of any bond that you may have posted to ensure your appearance at trial.

If you are found Guilty, you will usually be sentenced the same day. If the judge doesn't sentence you in the same breath, you should ask him if you can speak on the subject of *mitigation*. This is a term lawyers use when they hope the judge will be lenient after considering all the extenuating circumstances involved. Factors to be mentioned in mitigation include a good prior driving record (if such is the case); bad weather and/or road conditions; low volume of traffic; and the unlikelihood that you will commit another violation in the future.

Various kinds of sentences are meted out in traffic court. Depending on the severity of your crimes and your past record, the sentences imposed in traffic cases can be anything from a fine to a jail term, from points on your record to the loss of your driver's license. The judge may impose a sentence and suspend all or part of it, provided that you meet various conditions he specifies. A typical condition is that you not have a similar violation for a certain period of time, such as one year. (If you violate this condition, you are liable for the full amount of the suspended sentence plus whatever may result from the second offense.) A suspended sentence will appear on your record like any other sentence. Occasionally the judge will either suspend the sentence or even dismiss the case if you agree to attend a traffic violator's school.

Appeals

It is seldom feasible to appeal a traffic conviction. Appeals are often costly and time-consuming. Generally you'll need the services—at least the advice—of an experienced attorney. Even if you choose to proceed without an attorney, you'll have to pay a filing fee and wait a fair amount of time before your appeal is heard. Moreover, judges won't take kindly to a frivolous appeal; you should be determined that your case is legitimate—that there was a serious miscarriage of justice at the lower court trial—before appealing. This means that there was a legal errror of some kind, and not that the judge chose to believe the officer rather than you. The only possible exception to the advice against appealing is if you have lost your license and driving is vital to your work.

Using the Federal
Government

16

Congressmen and Bureaucrats

*The principal business of government is to
further and promote human striving.*
   —Wilbur L. Cross
   (former Governor of Connecticut)

THE image many Americans have of the federal government
—one that may not be far from accurate—is that of a big,
bungling, boondoggling bureaucracy. When forced to deal
with its maze of departments, divisions, agencies, and offices,
citizens frequently come away feeling confused, frustrated,
and inadequate. There are some three million federal employees, whose essential humanity is often camouflaged by
steadfast adherence to regulations and covered by an ava-
lanche of paper work. Public servants are often rightly perceived as little more than pencil-pushing automatons, caught
forever in a colossal entanglement of red tape. The best of
them are regarded as diligent drones, the worst as pompous
and overpaid parasites.

The barriers that exist between the 225 million Americans
who aren't in Washington and those few who are frequently
seem like iron curtains. This is especially true for individuals
(as opposed to interest groups) who need or want something
done by "the feds." It is not unusual even for skilled attorneys

to encounter stupefying obstacles when dealing with government bureaucracies—some of which seem to be in direct competition with one another. Trying to reach a bureaucrat by
telephone can be a time-consuming ordeal: he is likely to be
"in a meeting," "on a long-distance call," "at a conference,"
"out to lunch," "out of town," "out of the office," or, ultimately,
"no longer with us." Diligent and conscientious public servants,
on the other hand, are frequently shunted aside and neutral-
ized by their own agencies.

Congress itself, maintain many critics, is too obese, arthritic,
parochial, and nonresponsive or overresponsive. Visitors to the
House and Senate galleries often want to know, "Where is
everybody? Why aren't the others here to listen to what he is
saying?"

In fact, members of the House and Senate spend only a
small portion of their time in the two chambers. Most of their
days are consumed in committee hearings or briefings, legislative lunches or organized dinners. A considerable amount of
time is devoted to meeting with constituents.

There is even less understanding about one of the most important functions filled by elected public officials—that of
ombudsmen, problem-solvers for individuals who have been
ignored, trampled upon, or otherwise shabbily treated by the
government. It's called "case work," and it covers a wide
variety of dilemmas: your Social Security check has been
stopped or stolen and you have no other means of support; an
agency writes and says that you are no longer disabled and
your compensation has been terminated; an IRS man, without
advance notice, snaps a lock on the front door of your business; your visa has expired and cannot be extended, so you
must leave the country.

The cases of individual hardship inflicted by government
practice or neglect are legion and, it seems, never-ending.
While the work load and dedication of individual Representatives and Senators may vary, it is fair to say that most congressional offices devote as much as 40 percent of their resources to

resolving conflicts between their constituents and the government. Yet many people are unaware that the service is even available, much less that it often provides relief.

The easiest and best way to get what you want out of Washington is to know someone with both power and information. Perhaps even more fundamental is to recognize that such resources are not limited to the landed gentry or useful only to established interest groups. The fact is that most Americans have at least several agent/advocates in Washington who are virtually ideal problem-solvers—who work long hours, pursue difficult situations to reasonable resolutions, and do not charge for their services. They are skilled at penetrating the red tape of bureaucracy. Indeed, this chapter could conceivably begin and end with one thought: in an almost endless variety of circumstances, *getting what you want out of Washington means calling or writing your Congressman or Senator.* This is frequently the first, foremost, and last action necessary.

A surprising number of Americans don't realize that it's unnecessary to have a special relationship with their elected representatives—either by party affiliation or past campaign support, or through family or friends—in order to get things done on their behalf.

Most calls or letters will receive at least some response, usually quick and courteous. It is unlikely that the Senator or Congressman himself will handle the problem, but someone from his usually well-trained staff of caseworkers probably will. Even mass mailings of postcards advocating a particular position will often be answered, if there are return addresses. (The only correspondence that is unlikely to be answered is hate mail.)

Not only do letter writers get a response, they receive the personal attention of a variety of aides. First, the assistant assigned to the issues covered in the letter (for example, military matters) reviews it. His draft answer must be approved by the chief legislative assistant, who in turn shows it to the chief administrative assistant. The Senator or Congressman gives final approval.

Writing your Representative is generally a more effective approach than phoning. If the letter describes a problem you are having with the federal government, make sure it is stated clearly and concisely. It is important to provide all the relevant details—name, address, phone numbers (day and evening), Social Security number. Then give a complete chronological explanation of the problem, including the agencies with which contact has already been made, the names and titles of those government employees to whom questions were presented, their responses to date, and exactly what corrective action you seek. In some cases, written inquiries are a legal necessity: the Privacy Act of 1974 prohibits federal agencies from releasing information about an individual without his authorization in writing.

Letters are most helpful when they reflect a balanced and realistic grasp of a particular issue—when they thoughtfully present the way things are and offer a feasible solution or another option. Be sure to include copies of all relevant documents, including correspondence with the agency in question.

In calling a congressional office with a problem or opinion, it is equally important to supply all pertinent information. Think about what you want to say before you pick up your telephone. Make notes if necessary. Organize your thoughts. If you are seeking a copy of a bill or want to know its status in the House or Senate, be as clear and specific as possible (provide both a description of the bill and its number, if you know it).

Take advantage of the service offered by an elected official's local (district) offices. They are equipped to deliver messages directly to the Washington headquarters—and in many cases can save you the cost of a long-distance telephone call.

A Senator himself ordinarily becomes involved in a constituent's problem only when his staff is unable to handle it. On occasion, real political clout is needed: a cabinet officer will generally not talk to a staff member—nor will another Senator or a high White House official.

It's also wise to understand that, with over four hundred Representatives and a hundred Senators, the quality of service from office to office is likely to differ. Some are simply better than others. In gross terms, however, the great majority of legitimate problems submitted by constituents are solved—sooner or later—to their satisfaction.

17

Privacy and Information

The makers of our Constitution . . . conferred,
as against the Government, the right to be let
alone—the most comprehensive of rights and
the right most valued by civilized men.
　　　　　　　　　　—Justice Louis D. Brandeis
　　　　　　　　　　OLMSTEAD v. U.S.

TODAY, no matter who you are or what you do, the federal government is almost certain to have information about you or about some subject that interests you. This presents you with two separate problems: how do you get the information you want, and how do you prevent the government from disseminating private information about you to others who have no legitimate interest in it? On the information-gathering side, the problem is made more difficult because of bureaucratic inertia, a tendency on the part of government officials to treat government files as their own, and a desire by officials at all levels of government to want to hide information that may be embarrassing to them.

Sometimes government secrecy is in the public interest. Surely, no one would suggest that the invasion plan for the Battle of Normandy should have been released to *The New*

York Times before D-day, or that the leader of an organized
crime ring should have access to all the FBI files on him.
Similarly, there are often good reasons for one federal agency
to ask another agency for information about you—such as
when you apply for a job. Who's to decide whether disclosure
or secrecy is in the public interest?

Not, says Congress, the bureaucracy itself.

Fortunately, Congress has sought to protect American citizens from unwarranted intrusion into their private affairs, as
well as from the wrongful withholding of information that is
rightfully theirs. Under the Freedom of Information Act
(FOIA) of 1966 and the Privacy Act of 1974, the limits of federal information dissemination have been strictly defined.

Through the Freedom of Information Act various interested
individuals have gained access to material as diverse as Justice
Department files (concerning corporate mergers), records of
the Commodity Futures Trading Commission (pertaining to
the Chicago Board of Trade's application to trade future contracts in gold coins), and internal policy memoranda of the
Social Security Administration (suggesting guidelines for deciding disability claims). Many others have been able to review personal data gathered about them by the Federal
Bureau of Investigation or the Central Intelligence Agency.

On the other hand, the Privacy Act has served to stem the
flow of information which agencies may have about citizens to
agencies or persons not entitled to have access to it.

Because the government's store of information is so enormous and the right of access not absolute, acquiring government records is an exercise in the arts of communication,
persuasion, and, on occasion, compromise. Many of the sensitive disclosures related above succeeded only after the seekers
had brought suit and obtained a court order.

The Freedom of Information Act

The FOIA is broadly applied. Though the FOIA has been
amended twice since its enactment in 1966, its basic structure

has remained unchanged. The Act applies to records held by any federal agency, which means any executive or military department, any government or government-controlled corporation, any establishment in the executive branch (including the Executive Office of the President), or any independent regulatory agency. It does *not* apply to Congress, to the judiciary, or to state agencies (although many states have their own FOIA, modeled after the federal law).

"Records" encompass many different kinds of data. Although the FOIA does not define *records*, it is clear that the term encompasses all documents—which the courts have extended to cover photographs, computer tapes, and union-authorization cards. Government records are divided into three categories. The first must automatically be published in the *Federal Register*, whether requested by a citizen or not. These include an agency's rules of procedure, its substantive regulations, information describing its organization, and other matters basic to the public's understanding of how it functions. The second category need not be published but must be available for public inspection and copying: final opinions and orders rendered by the agency in deciding cases, policy statements and interpretations not published in the *Federal Register*, and certain agency staff manuals. The third category covers almost all other records—which must be furnished upon request—and it engenders the most litigation. These records, if properly requested and *not statutorily exempt from disclosure*, must be made "promptly available" to the individual requesting them.

Nine kinds of records are exempt from disclosure. With a few exceptions, such as where another statute forbids disclosure, an agency may choose to waive an exemption and release the documents sought. The nine exemptions are for matters related to:

1. *National security.* Information deemed confidential—according to criteria established by an Executive Order

signed by the President—"in the interest of national security or foreign policy."

2. *Agency personnel practices.* Information relating "solely to the internal personnel rules and practices of an agency."

3. *A special statute.* Information specifically exempted from disclosure by a statute (other than the Privacy Act), provided that the statute either requires the matters be withheld from the public in such a manner as to leave no discretion, or that it establishes particular criteria for withholding.

4. *Trade secrets.* This exemption is designed to protect free enterprise by shielding from disclosure certain kinds of information voluntarily submitted to the government by businesses, if its release would harm their competitive position in the marketplace.

5. *Inter- and intra-agency memoranda.* This exemption is designed to permit agency personnel to exchange advice and ideas with one another without the stifling threat of publicity. Its criteria are not noted for their clarity.

6. *Personnel files.* Medical and similar files the disclosure of which would constitute a clearly unwarranted invasion of personal privacy.

7. *Law-enforcement and investigatory records.* Exempt if disclosure would interfere with law-enforcement proceedings, deprive an individual of a right to fair trial or impartial adjudication, constitute an unwarranted invasion of personal privacy, disclose the identity of a confidential source, disclose investigative techniques and procedures, or endanger the life or physical safety of law-enforcement personnel.

8. *Financial-institution data.* Data "contained in or related to examination, operating, or condition reports prepared by, on behalf of, or for the use of an agency responsible for the regulation or supervision of financial institutions" (i.e., about banks).

9. *Wells.* Geological and geophysical information (including maps) concerning wells.

Exemptions are not always clear-cut. Even a cursory review of these exemptions makes plain that their application to a particular FOIA request is not always clear. Hence the litigation. The simplest advice is that since the exemptions are sometimes vague and never obligatory unless made so by some other statute, they should not deter you from making an FOIA request. The agency will let you know if it wishes to claim an exemption.

When making a FOIA request, you have three preliminary concerns. Three statutory provisions must be kept in mind when requesting records under the Freedom of Information Act:

1. The request must "reasonably describe" the records sought.
2. It must conform to the rules and procedures of the agency involved.
3. The agency may charge a fee to cover the cost of copying the records and for time spent searching for them. However, if release of the records "can be considered as primarily benefitting the general public," the agency must release them free of charge. Under no circumstances may the agency charge for time spent reviewing documents for possible exemptions.

Find out where the records are kept. An agency has no obligation to track down and release records over which it has no control. Therefore, before spending the time and money on a request, the seeker should be reasonably certain which agency has the records. If it is found that the records are not in the agency's possession, your request will be denied. Note that many agencies have more than one branch, and some requests will not be forwarded even within an agency unless you ask. Moreover, if the request is forwarded, time has been lost.

The following methods are useful in tracking down appropriate agencies and branches in the event of uncertainty:

1. Call the agencies you think are the likely custodians of the records in question. Most if not all of them have public information (or FOIA) departments, which should be able to tell you if the types of records you seek are of the type usually kept, or if a branch office or another agency should have them.
2. Consult the United States Government Manual. Revised yearly, this handbook lists all federal government agencies and describes their respective functions. It is available in libraries or from the Superintendent of Documents, U.S. Government Printing Office, Washington, D.C. 20402, for about $15.
3. Understand that regional offices usually maintain an agency's *working files*—those with facts pertaining to specific operations. If the information you seek is general or policy-making in nature, the national headquarters of the agency is more likely to have what you want.
4. Determine the age of the information you seek. If the files are old (compiled and closed several years ago), they might be stored at the National Archives or at its regional records centers.
5. Contact a regional Federal Information Center. Almost every state has one.

Try to assess the agency's reputation. You may find that more than one agency possesses the records you want. In such a circumstance, further investigation would be to your advantage: Which agency has the better reputation for cooperation? Your elected representative might well know the answer to that question. Is one of the agencies subject to an exemption— for example, a statute prohibiting it from releasing the records —while the other is not? A call to the agency should provide a quick answer. Another preliminary but important consideration is whether there is any possibility that the target agency will lose custody of the records in the near future. If your FOIA request was received after such a transfer has taken place, you're out of luck: the agency cannot honor it even if the records sought are not exempt from disclosure. But if the records were transferred *after* your request was received, your request is still legally enforceable.

Determine the agency's FOIA rules and procedures. By now you should know exactly what material you are looking for and which agency is likely to have it. But since the statute requires that you conform your request to the rules of that agency (so long as it complies with the FOIA itself), you must consult those rules. Agency procedural rules are first published in the *Federal Register* (which appears daily); they are then compiled and updated in the *Code of Federal Regulations*. Typically, they include a schedule of fees, a list of items which must be included in the request in order to locate the documents, notification if the request must be in writing, and other pertinent procedural requirements. The *Code of Federal Regulations* is composed of fifty sections (called "titles"), many of which contain more than one volume. (If you plan to deal with an agency on a regular basis, you may wish to purchase the title pertaining to that agency from the Superintendent of Documents. They cost from $7 to $10 per volume. If you do not wish to buy a *CFR* title, you can obtain the rules from the agency itself or consult the *Code* in a library which carries it.)

Put the request in writing. Asking for information by letter ensures that there will be a written record in the event misunderstandings arise. Also, many people express themselves with more clarity on paper, and that is important if you want your request to be processed efficiently.

Include a precise description of the records you seek. A description will be *legally* sufficient if it is clear enough to enable a professional employee of the agency, familiar with the subject area, to locate the records "with a reasonable amount of effort." As a practical matter, simple and precise requests get the quickest and least expensive agency response. Large-scale requests (e.g., "all records concerning DDT") will obviously take up more of the agency's time—time for which you will pay unless the agency has agreed to waive fees. You might fare better if you break down such large demands into a series of smaller, more specific requests. It is also a good idea to make direct, personal contact with agency personnel before sending the letter, to ascertain how it can best be worded in order to expedite the search.

Determine whether the materials you seek have been previously released under the FOIA. If so, the agency should have no difficulty finding the records so long as you can provide the name of the person (or organization) to whom they were disclosed and/or the date. Each release is given an identifying number: if you can supply it, so much the better. Note in your letter that a prior release should eliminate search fees.

State the reason you want to have the records. The FOIA does not require this, but explaining your need for the documents might persuade the agency to waive fees if there is a chance that disclosure could be considered as "primarily benefitting the general public." An explanation of need might also avoid an exemption if it demonstrates that the benefit to the public resulting from disclosure outweighs the benefit advanced by strict application of the exemption. Finally, if your need for the material is immediate, an explanation of the urgency might prompt a quicker response.

Decide how much you are willing to incur in fees. Generally, fees should be arranged in advance: you should have an idea of what it will cost, and the agency should have an idea how much you are willing to pay. Some agencies, in fact, require a portion of the fees to be paid in advance. If you do not want to spend above a specific amount, indicate your limit in the request letter. If the agency estimates search and copying costs will exceed your ceiling, you might be able to narrow your request or reduce copying costs by asking to review the material in person once it is found, to save on copying charges for useless documents. Some agencies maintain reading rooms in which you can make such a review.

Establish your authority. Indicate in your request that it is pursuant to the Freedom of Information Act and that you are cognizant of your rights under that law, including the right to nonexempt portions of exempt files if such portions can be segregated from the rest of the file; the right to a response within the statutory time limits; and the right to appeal an adverse decision.

Your envelope should be addressed to the agency from which data are sought, with this notation: "Attention: Freedom of Information/Privacy Act Unit."

The statutory time limits: by when must the agency respond? From the time it receives your request, the agency has ten days (not counting weekends or legal holidays) to inform you whether it will comply with your request or claim an exemption. The agency can extend this period up to ten more days if it can demonstrate "unusual circumstances." Such an extension, however, must likewise be claimed in a written notification to you.

If a time period has expired and the agency has not responded, you can appeal to the agency's chief officer, institute a legal action in federal court, or wait a bit longer. Displaying some patience will often be the best strategy. At such an early stage in the process, you need not view the agency as adversary. Keeping open lines of communication, by telephone or letter, will enable you to determine the cause of the delay, establish a tentative decision date, and clarify the request if a misunderstanding has occurred. The agency may tell you it has been forced to delay in order to satisfy the demands of another statute—especially when the information requested has been submitted to the government by a third party (such as a private corporation): some statutes or rules require notice to the third party before data are released. On the other hand, if

it appears to you that an agency is stalling for no legitimate
reason, it is important that you understand your full rights of
appeal.

**If the agency says the records are unavailable, destroyed, or
not in existence, do not give up.** Such responses need not end
the inquiry. Call the agency or send another letter. If the
records have been sent someplace else, ask where and when. If
the agency claims the records don't exist, state any reasons you
might have indicating the contrary. (It is always possible,
given the size of the bureaucracy, that other agency personnel
are more familiar with the type of material requested than the
individual who processed your initial request). Ask about the
nature and scope of the search. Make the agency convince you
that it made a genuine effort to locate the records sought. If
you're told the files were destroyed, ask when: it is illegal to
destroy records once they have been requested. In short, if you
believe that the agency might be mistaken or evasive, don't
give up. Remember that public servants are your employees.
Treat them fairly, and expect good service.

**When the agency responds by denying all or part of your
request, consider an appeal.** If some or all of the requested
materials are withheld, you still have the right to appeal to the
head of the agency (or to whomever he has appointed to
handle FOIA appeals). The letter of denial from the agency is
important: it should state that you have such a right; indicate
to whom the appeal should be addressed; and provide details
as to which materials are being withheld, which exemptions
are being claimed, and the names and titles of the persons
responsible for the decision to withhold the records. The letter
should also state what fees you owe (and why they were not
waived if so requested).

Your appeal should also be by letter. Make sure it is sent
within the time limit set by the agency's regulations (usually,
thirty days). You must make certain it is addressed to the
correct official, states clearly the agency decision which you'd

like to challenge (including the dates of request and denial, the records sought, and any other relevant information), and gives reasons you think the denial was wrong.

Just as with the initial request letter, you should also establish your legal authority: that you are making an appeal pursuant to your rights under the Freedom of Information Act, that you expect a reply within the statutory time limit (twenty working days from the date the appeal is received), and that you have a right to a definitive list of both documents retrieved and those withheld (under specified exemptions).

Even at the appellate stage, informal lines of communication should be maintained with the agency. Personal contact can move the process along to your greater satisfaction, as well as promote a spirit of compromise. Remember that, although agency personnel are supposed to be at your service, they should be treated as civilly as you would have them treat you.

If you feel you have been charged excessive fees, you can appeal the fee assessment using the same procedures as for an appeal of a denial.

If the appeal fails, consider going to court. If the agency refuses to change an initial adverse decision, or fails to respond within the twenty-day time limit, you have the right to take the matter to court. Before rushing into litigation, however, consider two alternatives:

1. Write to the Freedom of Information Clearinghouse (P.O. Box 19367, Washington, D.C. 20036), which sometimes can give advice or assistance not otherwise available.
2. Ask your Congressman or Senator for assistance.

If you decide to sue, you should probably hire a lawyer to help (although you are not required by law to do so). Attorneys are not cheap, but if you go to court and win, the government must pay your lawyer's reasonable fees.

The Privacy Act

The Privacy and Information Acts overlap. The FOIA enables you to obtain federal agency records; the Privacy Act protects you from unwarranted disclosures about your private life. It also provides a separate means of obtaining records about yourself which is in addition to, and in some instances broader than, your rights under the FOIA. Also, the Privacy Act provides a means to have erroneous information in your files corrected.

The Privacy Act extends to any records that pertain to you individually (e.g., your tax or personnel file). Such personal records maintained by the federal government cannot be released to anyone "except pursuant to a written request by, or with the prior written consent of, the individual to whom the record pertains." And they can be sent to another agency only if the other agency uses them for certain authorized purposes.

Conversely, the Privacy Act provides that an agency must permit any individual, upon his request, to gain access to and copy any part of his or her personal records. Copying costs— but not search costs—can be charged to the individual making the request. Citizens also have the right to demand that their records be amended if they are not "accurate, timely, relevant, or complete."

As with the FOIA, Congress saw fit to provide for certain exceptions to the Privacy Act. For example, the Central Intelligence Agency (or any other agency whose principal function is criminal-law enforcement) can deny access to personal records —but cannot exempt itself from the requirement of prior written consent. In addition, any federal agency can exempt certain records from access: those already under the FOIA's national security exemption; investigative material compiled for civil or criminal law-enforcement purposes; records maintained in connection with protective services accorded the President and other officials; records which are required by statute to be purely statistical in nature and use; material compiled solely for the purpose of determining suitability for federal civilian employment, promotion, military service, federal contracts, or access to classified information (but only to the extent that disclosure would reveal the identity of a confidential source); and testing data used solely for appointment or promotion in the civil or armed services (the disclosure of which would impair objectivity or fairness).

Finally, federal agencies are not required to provide access to information compiled in reasonable anticipation of a civil action or proceeding.

Requests under the Privacy Act should be made in writing. There are numerous similarities between the data-request processes of the Privacy and Information Acts. The request need not be in writing (unless the agency specifically requires it), but a written demand is best for expediting the process. The request must conform to the agency's regulations, which appear in the *Code of Federal Regulations* or can be obtained from the agency itself. You must lodge the request with the agency which has control over the records. Costs should be made clear in advance; fee schedules are listed in the agency's regulations. The more specific and clear the request, the faster the response.

Mention both the FOIA and the Privacy Act. In asserting your right of access to the records, refer to both laws as your legal authority: many agencies will process a request under whichever statute provides greater access (if the records are exempt under the Privacy Act, they might still be available under the FOIA). If the agency you have approached does not subscribe to this policy—and some don't—it will let you know. You must limit your demands, at least initially, to what's available under the companion statute.

Identify yourself. To protect your records from unauthorized release, you must identify yourself to the satisfaction of the agency. At minimum, you should be prepared to offer your full name (including any other names used during the period when the records were compiled), your address, and a notarized signature. If you want to inspect the documents in person, identification cards may be necessary.

Identify the records you seek. The Act requires that each agency publish in the *Federal Register* a list of its records systems which contain information pertaining to individuals. These lists have been compiled in *Protecting Your Right to Privacy: Digest of Systems of Records*, available in libraries or from the Superintendent of Documents, U.S. Government Printing Office, Washington, D.C. 20402. Your request will be easier for the agency to process if you indicate to which particular records system you want access.

Know the time limits. There is no statutory time limit within which the agency must respond under the Privacy Act. The Office of Management and Budget, which is authorized to create guidelines for the implementation of the Act, has provided that an agency "should" respond within ten working days and provide access (if no exemption is asserted) within thirty working days. OMB guidelines provide for further time to comply if the agency advises the requester that there is "good cause" for delay. (The "OMB Guidelines" appear in the *Federal Register*, Volume 40, beginning at page 28949, July 9, 1979.)

Administrative appeal is not a matter of right. The Privacy Act does not require that there be an administrative appeal in the event you are dissatisfied with the agency's response (or lack of one). Whether there is an intra-agency appeal process depends on the agency involved. But if your demands are not met, the Privacy Act also provides for the right to sue.

The right to amend personal records is yours. You have the right to request that your records be amended if you discover, upon reviewing them, that they are not accurate, timely, relevant, or complete. The agency must acknowledge such a request within ten working days, and must determine its merits "promptly." If the request is denied, you have the right to appeal to the head of the agency or the appeals officer he has appointed. The agency's decision on appeal must be made within thirty working days, unless the agency has "good cause" for delay.

Hiring a Lawyer

18

Hiring a Lawyer

*For a crust of bread he can be hired either to
keep silence or to speak.*
                    —Cato, NOCTES ATTICAE

THERE is no right way to hire a lawyer, any more than
there's only one way to engage a painter or to find a doctor.
But there are techniques for being a wise shopper. Some of
them follow:

Recommendations of friends can be helpful. A great many
people pick lawyers by word of mouth—that is, they go to an
attorney who's been recommended by a friend or relative, or
who has a good reputation in the community.

Some lawyer referral services are not as good as others. If
you're new in a community, you might want to contact a lawyer referral service. Practically every bar association maintains
such a service. The best ones seek to match people with particular legal problems and attorneys qualified to handle them.
Ignore those which handle you strictly on a first-come, first-
serve basis. The services vary from one bar association to
another. Most require a simple contact either by telephone or

in writing. (Numbers and addresses can usually be found in the classified telephone directory under "Lawyer Referral Service.")

The stated goals of referral services sound noble—but the proof is in the pudding. The stated philosophy and purpose of one typical service are to supply needed general or legal information to persons who do not know if they have a legal problem or who do not know a lawyer to consult; to locate qualified lawyers who have listed themselves in various kinds of legal practices; to remove financial barriers to legal services for poorer people; to monitor costs, services, and client satisfaction; to filter out those cases not needing legal services and provide information about other available social services; and to coordinate activities with other legal service organizations.

All of this sounds very high-minded and public-spirited, but you'd be wise to screen prospective counsel carefully.

Legal Aid is still available, if you qualify. Despite cutbacks in federal funding, most communities still have some form of legal aid service available to low-income people. The functions performed may be limited, however, and the income ceilings may also have been raised. Because services and criteria vary so widely, it's best to contact your local legal aid agency (generally listed in the telephone book under "Legal Aid").

Many public-interest organizations provide legal services. Often they are in specialized areas of the law. Some of them can refer you to lawyers who are the most experienced and qualified in their fields.

Clinical programs of law schools can be helpful. Many law schools nowadays have specialized clinical programs (as, for example, in juvenile law or prisoner assistance). Check with the schools in your area to determine what clinics are available.

Prepaid legal services are similar to health-insurance plans. In the past, prepaid legal service plans usually have been available only to groups (such as labor unions, credit unions, and cooperatives). More recently, prepaid legal service plans have become available to individual consumers. Some of these plans are excellent. Others promised too much for too low a payment and have gone out of business. If you find a prepaid plan that interests you, inquire carefully about it. If you have questions about any specific plan, contact the National Resource Center for Consumers of Legal Services by calling (202) 659-8514 or writing to National Resource Center, 1302 Eighteenth Street NW, Washington, D.C. 20036.

Many lawyers now advertise. In compiling your list of lawyers, you can also look at the advertisements in the newspaper (although advertising by lawyers is relatively new and used by relatively few attorneys). If your problem is routine, this may be a good method of finding a lawyer who will provide a service for a fixed fee. Legal clinics, which work on a volume basis, using standardized forms with the assistance of trained nonlawyers called paralegals, are likely to advertise frequently. They are often able to handle routine legal problems at lower costs. Some of them give free initial consultations.

These methods should enable you to find the names of several lawyers with experience with your kind of problem. Call and talk with several of them before making your first appointment.

Talk to the Lawyer of Your Choice

The following suggestions have been excerpted and adapted with permission from *Finding and Hiring a Lawyer*, published by the Citizens' Advisory Committee of the District of Columbia Bar:

Phoning the lawyer's office. Before you make an appointment, call the offices of the lawyers on your list to get more information. When you call the lawyer's office, find out the name of the person with whom you are speaking. Describe your problem and ask briefly, but clearly:

1. "Does the lawyer (or "Do you . . .") have experience with this kind of problem?"
2. "Does the lawyer charge for an initial interview?" If so, "How much?"
3. If you believe your problem is routine, "Does the lawyer have a standard fee for this kind of problem? What does that standard fee cover?"
4. If your problem is more complicated or the lawyer does not have a standard fee, "What is the lawyer's hourly fee?"
5. "Does the lawyer provide a written agreement describing fees and the services provided for the fees?"

Keep a list of the information and think about the answers you receive from the lawyers. Then call back to make an appointment with the attorney whose answers satisfied you the most. Don't be embarrassed: you are entitled to ask these questions and receive answers to them before you hire a lawyer.

The first face-to-face interview. Plan to go to the first interview with an open mind. You do not have to decide to employ the lawyer you are interviewing until you have had time to think about the interview. Do not be rushed into signing a retainer agreement.

A lawyer works for you. He or she should be genuinely interested in your problem and in giving you the best possible advice. The lawyer may not be able to accomplish everything you wish because of the facts or the law that applies in your case. Many times a good lawyer will advise you to avoid court action. A lawyer should be able to explain, in terms you can understand, what he or she hopes to accomplish for you and how he or she plans to do it. Keep this in mind as you reflect on your impressions of your contacts with the lawyer and his or her staff.

How to work with a lawyer. Be organized in presenting your concerns to the lawyer. Lawyers spend years in law school and in law practice learning, among other things, how to approach a problem in a logical, well-organized manner. Most lawyers respond better to clients who are well organized in interviews and phone conversations.

Remember also, a lawyer's time is his or her income. Be punctual for your interview and try to be unemotional in explaining your problem. When you go to the meeting, it is important to bring with you:

1. A written summary or detailed notes outlining your problem
2. Names, addresses, and phone numbers of all parties and witnesses and their lawyers and insurance companies, if you know them
3. All documents which you have received from lawyers or a court or which may otherwise be important, for example: receipts, contracts, medical bills, repair estimates, checks, etc. (Some lawyers will ask you to deliver written materials in advance of your first interview in order to review them.)

The cost of the interview. If you first spoke with someone else about the appointment, confirm the cost of the interview with the lawyer. Many charge for the initial interview at their usual hourly rate. In other cases, a reduced initial consultation fee may pay for only a short time with the lawyer. Make sure you understand the cost if the interview is going to take more time.

The lawyer's experience. You will want to check on the lawyer's experience. Not all lawyers are experienced, expert, and efficient with every subject. Usually, the hourly fee of an experienced lawyer is higher than that of an inexperienced lawyer, but if the experienced lawyer is more efficient, the total cost may be less for you and the results better in the long run. However, a young lawyer may be more interested in your case, especially if it is routine, and may be more effective. In any case, avoid the lawyer with a high hourly fee who is not experienced with your type of problem.

You have the right to know about the lawyer's experience. If your case is going to involve a trial or administrative hearing, be sure the lawyer is experienced with these proceedings. Whomever you decide to hire, you should feel confident in him or her.

If you are working with a law firm, ask who will actually be working on your case and decide if you should talk directly with that person. If someone other than a partner, for example a young lawyer (called an *associate* in a large firm), or a nonlawyer, is doing the work, you should know about it and the cost of the service should be less. Here are some questions that you should ask:

"Will you actually be working on my case, or should I talk with another person who will be doing the work on my case?"

"Have you had experience with this type of problem before? How recently? How often? What was involved?"

If your problem is a common legal problem, like a divorce or employment discrimination case, you can ask: "What percentage of your practice is devoted to this kind of problem?"

Your role in the case. You have the right to be an active participant if you want to. Explain to the lawyer what you would like your role to be. People experienced in dealing with lawyers often put in a substantial amount of time assisting the lawyers in gathering evidence, lining up witnesses, and, after receiving the lawyer's advice, making final decisions about their cases. More active clients generally receive better legal service. If you can, plan to take an active role working with your lawyer. If this is what you want to do, make it clear to the lawyer at the first interview.

At the interview, tell the lawyer that you want to:

1. Receive a copy of all documents, letters, etc., received or written in your case at the lawyer's out-of-pocket cost, or to have these documents made available to you at his or her office
2. Be informed about all developments in the case
3. Be consulted before decisions are made in the case and, in important instances, to make the decisions yourself

Think about how the lawyer responded to your questions, about his or her experience, and whether you will be able to work with the lawyer in the way you would like.

If you are satisfied with the interview so far, tell the lawyer everything about your problem, including facts which may be unfavorable to you. There are strict rules which prohibit lawyers from repeating to anyone what you say to them unless you confess ongoing or planned criminal activity. Remember, your lawyer can give you a realistic explanation of what can be accomplished only if you are completely honest.

If you wish, you can ask the lawyer to explain both the positive and the negative aspects of the case.

A timetable for your case. Next, ask the lawyer if a timetable can be established for your case. Find out what the lawyer will be doing, and when and how you will be back in touch with each other. Most cases have a legal time limit, called the *statute of limitations*, before which they must be filed or you will lose all your rights.

Regarding a timetable, you should ask:

1. "Can you give me a list of events that are likely to occur in my case, and a timetable for them?"
2. "Will you give me your best estimate of how long this case will take to complete?"
3. "What will you do next?"
4. "Is there a statute of limitations on the case? When does it expire?"
5. "When will we talk again?"

Fees and payments. Crucial to you and your lawyer's future comfort and confidence in each other is the establishment of a clear, fully understood fee and payment arrangement. Establish a fee arrangement which you clearly understand, even if your lawyer is a friend or says he or she is taking the case on a reduced-fee basis. Disagreements about fees are a very common source of dissatisfaction between lawyers and clients.

Fee arrangements vary from lawyer to lawyer, reflecting a few basic approaches. Only some of the details on fees and payments listed below will apply to your case:

At the interview, ask the lawyer to bill you on a regular basis as his or her time charges mount, so that you will never be surprised by the total size of the bill you receive. You can ask that the lawyer not exceed a specified amount of time devoted to your case or money spent on your case without first obtaining your permission. *Clients are entitled to itemized bills showing the work done and disbursements made,* before having to pay a lawyer.

Plan to reread this section before you go to your first appointment. Read it again after you have met with the attorney for the first time, to be sure you understand how you and the attorney are handling fee and payment arrangements. Call your lawyer if you have any questions.

Written agreements. It is important that you and your lawyer enter into a written agreement, a contract, setting forth the lawyer's charges as well as what services the lawyer expects to perform for that payment. Presently, most agreements provide only for the fee to be paid by the client. Ask your attorney also to list what he or she will do in exchange for your payment. (Consumers Union publishes a model form, which can give you an idea of the kind of information that can be provided by a written agreement; write for "Lawyer's Questionnaire," Consumers Union, 1146 19th Street NW, Washington, D.C. 20036.)

Standard ·fees. Some attorneys and legal clinics offer fixed or standard fees for routine legal problems, such as drafting a simple will, probating an estate, handling an uncontested divorce with no property or custody issues, or executing an uncomplicated real estate settlement, etc. To see who offers standard fees for their services, you can check advertisements in the newspapers or listings in a Lawyers' Register or Directory, if your local bar association maintains one.

If your problem is uncomplicated, ask your lawyer to let you have, immediately if possible, an estimate of the total cost of the case, including expenses in excess of his or her fee. Then you can plan realistically to meet this financial obligation.

Expenses *not* covered in the fee. Lawyers usually expect to be reimbursed for expenses that they incur in connection with the client's case. These may include travel costs, meals away from home, long-distance telephone calls, and postage and copying costs, to name a few examples. Be sure to discuss with your lawyer any expenses for which you may be charged that are not included in the fee, and an estimate of how much they may be.

More complicated cases—hourly charges. Many attorneys bill on an hourly basis. Their fees vary from $20 per hour to over $100 for each hour of the attorney's time. You can ask about a reduced rate if you find a lawyer you want to employ but whose fees are higher than you can afford. Again, ask your lawyer to let you have, immediately or as soon as possible, an estimate of what the total cost will be.

Lawyers usually bill for all time spent on a case, including time spent talking with a client on the telephone, time at the courthouse waiting to appear in court, etc.

Lawyers cannot always estimate how many hours a case will take. If you agree to an hourly arrangement, your written agreement should include a provision requiring that the lawyer not exceed a specified amount of time or money without obtaining your permission. Insist that the lawyer keep you advised every month, or more often if necessary, of the number of hours that he or she is spending on your case. If you have any questions about this, you are also entitled to a more detailed written explanation of how those hours were spent.

Retainer agreements. Some lawyers require an advance fee, called a retainer. Ask the attorney what is covered by the retainer fee.

A retainer fee usually represents a number of hours of the attorney's time at his or her usual hourly rate. If the number of hours of the lawyer's work on your case exceeds the amount covered by the retainer, he or she will bill you for the additional charges. In that case, you and your lawyer should also agree beforehand that a refund will be made if the attorney does not spend as much time as has been covered by the retainer. You should agree on how fees and billing and payment arrangements will be handled for any amount in excess of the retainer.

Occasionally, the retainer is for a flat fee, to cover the entire cost of the lawyer's services regardless of the amount of time the lawyer spends. In that case, you may be unable to get a refund from your advance payment even if the lawyer does very little work, but you will not owe more if the lawyer underestimates the time it will take. Also determine if the fee paid for the initial consultation will be included in the retainer.

Be sure to get a receipt for fees paid in cash or by money order.

Contingency fee cases. In accident or personal injury cases, and in some other instances, some lawyers will agree to accept as their entire fee a percentage of the money you receive if you win the case. If no recovery is made in the case, the client usually pays the lawyer only for expenses incurred in the case, like court fees. This is called a *contingency fee* arrangement.

Contingency fee contracts are like other contracts, except that if you don't get something in writing, you can be virtually certain that your lawyer will tell you that his interpretation is the customary one—and it will invariably favor him, not you. Thus, the client is usually expected to pay the costs of the lawsuit and other items such as medical expenses out of his or her share, not out of the lawyer's.

It is not unusual to find a lawyer willing to take his share *after* the expenses of litigation, but not many will agree to do the same thing with medical and other expenses. But there is no harm in trying. Most important of all, be sure you understand precisely how the lawyer's fee will be computed before you sign the contingency fee agreement. (In many states, such agreements are required to be in writing, but even in the states that don't require this, you should insist on it.)

And when your lawyer proposes to settle your case, be sure you figure out precisely how much you will end up with after paying the lawyer's fee, court costs, and other expenses. You may decide that you are ending up with too little and your lawyer too much and decide not to settle. Remember, it is always your decision, not your lawyer's, on whether the settlement offer is a reasonable one.

You may wish to try to negotiate a contingency fee arrangement with your lawyer that differs from the usual, in which the lawyer is paid one fourth to one half of the recovery. For example, if your medical costs, salary lost, and case-related expenses have been high, you could suggest payment first of medical costs, salary lost, and case-related expenses and then assign a higher percentage of the remaining recovery to the lawyer.

Payments. At your first meeting with your lawyer, set out specific arrangements for payments. If you cannot pay more than a certain amount per month, be sure that ceiling is agreeable to the lawyer.

Be specific about billing, too. For example, specify if you want to be billed monthly or whenever your lawyer has spent a certain number of hours on your case. This should be included in your written fee agreement.

A small minority of attorneys charge interest on overdue bills. You should ask about this beforehand also.

Here is a checklist of questions related to fees and payments:

1. "Can you give me an estimate of how much this legal matter will cost?"
2. "Can we have a written fee agreement that sets forth not only my obligation to pay but also exactly what you will do for me?"
3. "How often will I be billed? Will you agree to let me know when a specific dollar amount of your time has been spent on my case, so that I can authorize further payments?"
4. "Can you estimate how much court costs, witness and deposition fees, and any other costs will be, aside from your fees? In what manner will I be required to pay these costs?"
5. "When will I have to pay?" (Explain to the lawyer the payment schedule which is best for you.)

Be sure you understand the cost of your legal services, and how fees are to be determined and billed. Reread this section on fees and payments after your first interview. Make sure you ask and understand the answers to any questions you may have before you agree to hire a lawyer.

The decision to hire a lawyer. Based on your first interview, you should consider the following factors before agreeing to hire a lawyer:

1. Personality—Do you get along well with and trust the person?
2. Experience—Has the lawyer had enough experience with your type of problem?
3. Could you communicate effectively with the lawyer? Was he or she clear and easy to understand?

4. Are fees reasonable in comparison with other lawyers' charges?
5. Did your lawyer give clear explanations of how she or he will let you know about progress in your case?

If you are not satisfied with this lawyer, do not hire him or her, but look elsewhere for legal help. If you are satisfied, a sound basis for working together has probably been established between you and your lawyer.

Problems with your lawyer. Even if you take all of these steps before hiring a lawyer, you still may be dissatisfied with the way he or she is conducting your case. A client has the right to discharge an attorney at any time, although once you are in court, a judge may not permit this change except for a very good reason. Likewise, an attorney has the right to resign from representation of a client, but once you are in court, the judge's permission is needed. You can change lawyers, but before doing so, remember that:

1. You should first talk with your attorney and try to straighten out the problem.
2. Other lawyers may be more reluctant to take your case if they know you have already had another lawyer, especially if your first lawyer has a good reputation.
3. You probably owe the lawyer for services already rendered. A new lawyer may have to repeat and charge you again for the work already done.
4. Your attorney may be unwilling to return legal papers he or she has unless the fee has been paid in full or your written fee agreement specifies that the attorney must do this if he or she stops representing you. The Consumers Union model form suggests language which may be used to establish this.
5. In a case where the court appoints the lawyer, for example in a criminal case where you cannot afford to pay for a lawyer, a judge must approve a change of lawyers.

6. If you have a dispute with your lawyer over a fee, contact your local bar association and ask if it has a fee arbitration program. Many bar associations maintain such a service, which is usually fair, fast—and much less expensive than going to court.

Conclusion. Trust your own common sense and feelings as you look for a lawyer, interview lawyers on the phone, and, finally, deal with your lawyer as a client. Asking your lawyer straightforwardly about anything you do not understand should help keep your relationship on a sound working basis.

Glossary/Appendices/
Bibliography

Glossary

FOLLOWING are brief definitions of legal terms used in this book. For more comprehensive explanations of these terms, consult either of the two leading law dictionaries—*Black's* (West Publishing Company, fifth edition, 1979) or *Ballentine's* (Lawyers' Cooperative, third edition, 1969)—or the multivolume series of judicial interpretations called *Words and Phrases* (West, updated annually).

Adoption • A procedure which establishes a parent/child relationship between persons not related by blood, and which terminates the rights and duties of the natural birth-parents

Affidavit • A statement under oath, usually required to be signed and sworn to before a notary public

Alimony • Money that one spouse pays to the other for financial support during a separation or after a legal divorce; generally expires upon remarriage of receiving spouse

Annulment • A judicial determination that a legal genuine marriage never took place

Antenuptial agreement • A premarital contract signed by a prospective husband and wife regarding such subjects as property and inheritance rights, division of household responsibilities, and payment of expenses

Assignment • The transfer to another person of one's entire interests, rights, and obligations in real or personal property, services, etc.

Assumable mortgages • Mortgage loans which may be transferred from seller to buyer, where the buyer continues to make payments at the interest rate (presumably lower) which prevailed at the time of the original mortgage

Attachment • A process by which a creditor, having obtained a

211

judgment, can take possession of a debtor's property, to sell it to pay the judgment

Attestation • Formalities associated with the act of witnessing a written legal document (such as a will or contract) at the request of the person signing the document

Balloon mortgage • A mortgage agreement under which only the interest is due during the term (usually short), with the entire principal due at the end of the term

Bankruptcy • The discharging of debts through an action in the federal courts, where all your nonexempt property is turned over to a trustee who tries to pay creditors as fully as possible; see "debt adjustment"

Bankruptcy trustee • The person appointed by a court to administer property for someone who is in a bankruptcy proceeding, to make sure that creditors receive what they are supposed to under the law

Bona fide occupational qualification (BFOQ) • A qualification which is considered to be necessary to perform a specific job

Capacity • The legal competency of a person to enter into a contract (e.g., whether one is of age and of sound mind)

Child support • Money a noncustodial parent pays toward maintenance of the children raised by the custodial parent; to be distinguished from alimony

Closed-end credit account • A credit account in which the balance must be paid before one is allowed to make additional purchases.

Codicil • An amendment adding to, deleting from, or modifying the terms of a will

Cohabitation agreement • A contract signed by two unmarried persons who are living together which outlines their mutual expectations regarding support and the division of property, household responsibilities, and expenses

Collateral • Property promised to a lender as security; that is, property which passes to the lender if there is a failure to pay a loan

Commission • Money paid to an agent; in real estate, a percentage of the selling price of the house, paid by the seller to the real-estate agent who found the buyer

Common property • Property held by two or more persons in common with each other; in marriage in a common-law system, each spouse owns whatever he or she earns; to be distinguished from *community property*

Community property • A legal concept regarding property owner-ship in marriage, that all property acquired by either spouse dur-ing marriage is owned by both of them, no matter whose name is on the legal title; currently in operation in the states of Arizona, California, Idaho, Louisiana, Nevada, New Mexico, Texas, and Washington; to be distinguished from *common property*

Condominium • A dwelling unit and a specified common area, generally part of a larger building or high-rise, which is owned (not rented) by the dweller

Consideration • The money, services, or property, or anything of value which one party gives up or gains as a result of a contract

Constructive eviction • A "legal fiction" that relieves a tenant of his or her obligations under a lease, allowing the tenant to aban-don the premises because conditions within the control of the landlord make the property unsuitable for occupancy

Contract • An agreement where certain promises or acts are ex-changed, and the parties are legally obligated to perform their part of the bargain

Cooperative housing • An apartment building or group of dwell-ings which is owned by a corporation, in which the lessees have shares of stock entitling them to live in a specific apartment or building

Corporation • An artificial entity with the legal power to do any-thing an individual or partnership can do, but which allows its owners (stockholders) to shield themselves from liability for debts and losses

Covenant • A promise; often a clause or condition in a contract

Cross-examination • Part of trial where one side asks questions of the opponent (or of a witness testifying for the opponent)

Custody • Usually the right to raise a minor child, and the duty to be responsible for such child

Debt adjustment • A method under the bankruptcy laws by which a debtor can retain all or most of his assets while paying current creditors over a period of time out of income

Decree • A court order, either interlocutory (temporary) or final

Deed • The document used to transfer title to real or personal property from a seller to a buyer

Deed of trust • Similar to a mortgage, except that usually a third party (not the lender or borrower) keeps legal title to the property until either a default occurs (in which case the lender may sell the property to repay the loan) or the borrower pays off his obligation

Default • Failure to pay an amount due, in either a mortgage or some other loan, whereby the lender gains certain rights to property (either by agreement of the parties or through court decree)

Defendant • The person sued by a plaintiff

Discrimination • In employment, favoring or disfavoring certain types of people

Domicile • A person's legal (permanent) home, although it need not be lived in (for example, a college student living in a dorm may have his domicile elsewhere)

Down payment • An outright cash payment which is made before money is borrowed

Easements • Rights that other people have in real estate allowing them to do certain things on a specific parcel of land, usually to cross over it to get to their property

Encumbrance • A legal right to or interest in property, which right or interest is owned by someone else—such as a tax lien, easement, zoning ordinance, or restrictive covenant; generally, encumbrances are "clouds on title" and diminish a property's value

Equitable distribution • A legal concept that allows a judge in a divorce proceeding to distribute property according to what he feels is fair, rather than according to who holds legal title

Escrow agreement • A document under which one or more parties designate a certain party (the escrow agent) to hold money (e.g., rental fees) until certain other events occur, such as the fulfillment of other obligations

Eviction • A legal action initiated by a landlord demanding that a tenant move out before expiration of a lease

Exclusive right to sell • A type of real-estate listing agreement in which only one agent is permitted to sell a piece of property

Exemption • Property that a debtor does not have to relinquish by virtue of bankruptcy proceedings

"Fault" divorce • A divorce based on grounds such as adultery, cruelty, or desertion, in which one of the parties is blamed for causing the divorce

Foreclosure • The process by which a bank (or other lender) can sell the property of a borrower who is in default, in order to pay off the money owed

Freedom of Information Act • A federal or state law which requires government agencies to disclose their records, with certain exceptions

Garnishment • A process by which a creditor may have a debtor's wages paid directly to him; must follow a court judgment obtained by creditor, and is generally limited to a modest percent of wages (typically 10%)

Grievance procedure • The terms of a particular employment contract which must be followed, if an employee has a complaint, before he can go to court

Guardian • A person legally given the power and duty to take care of someone who by age or disability is considered incapable of administering his own affairs

Holographic will • A will that is handwritten, dated, and signed by the testator, without witnesses or other formalities normally required by law

Implied warranty of habitability • An implied-by-law guarantee by landlord to tenant that the leased premises meet a reasonable standard

Incidental damages • Damages that occur as an indirect result of a product's deficiency or breach of a contract

Informed consent • The understanding that a doctor must obtain from a patient before treatment that the patient is fully aware of the possible risks and benefits of the medical procedure to be performed

Intestate succession • The statutory method of distributing the estate of a person who dies without a will

Joint tenancy • A form of joint ownership whereby property automatically transfers to the survivor (or survivors) upon the death of the other party

Joint venture • A form of business whereby two or more persons agree to act together to complete a single business transaction (rather than establish and operate a continuous business)

Judgment • A court decision that one person is entitled to certain rights, either to specific property or in more general terms

Jurisdiction • The power or authority of a court to decide a particular case

Landlord • One who rents premises to another (the tenant)

Lease • Contract between landlord and tenant, outlining the rights and obligations of each regarding the rented property

Letters testamentary • A legal document giving the estate's personal representative permission to transact matters on behalf of the estate

Lien • A legal method of enforcing a debt, whereby the property under lien cannot be sold or transferred before the creditor enforcing the lien has been paid

Limited partnership • A partnership in which some of the parties are liable only for a fixed amount of money, and are generally limited as well in their share of the profits

Listing agreement • An agreement between a seller of property and a real-estate agent, setting forth the contractual arrangement between them for advertising, showing, and selling the property

Minor • A person below the specific age of majority set by state law, who is afforded various protections by the law (such as not being liable for certain contracts); generally the age of majority is anywhere from eighteen to twenty-one years old, depending on the state (and, in some cases, depending on the circumstances)

Modification • Changing a contract after it has been signed

Mortgage/mortgagor/mortgagee • An agreement (the mortgage) between a buyer (the mortgagor) and a moneylender (the mortgagee), where the mortgagor borrows money to buy property—which in turn is used as collateral on the loan

Multiple listing agreement • An arrangement among real-state agents allowing each to show and sell houses which are listed by individual agents with a sharing of commissions

Negligence • A legal word used to describe a defendant's failure to act as a reasonable and prudent person under the circumstances, which failure directly causes injury to a plaintiff

"No-fault" divorce • A divorce in which neither party is blamed for causing the difficulty leading to the divorce

Partnership • A form of doing business in which two or more persons voluntarily agree to share both profits and losses from the operation of a business

Personal property • Assets other than real-estate, including household goods, stocks, cars, etc.

Personal representative • One appointed to handle the probate of the will or (where no will exists) to oversee the distribution of an estate according to intestate succession; often known as an executor

Petition • A formal document filed in a court of law outlining the pertinent facts of a situation and requesting the judge to give certain relief

Petitioner • One who initiates a court action

Plaintiff • The person who files a complaint against a defendant in a lawsuit

Points • In real estate, a percentage of the loan which a buyer must sometimes pay to a lender in order to obtain a mortgage; sometimes known as document-processing fees or discount points

Power of attorney • A written legal paper in which one appoints someone else as his agent to whom he gives either a general or limited authority to act in his behalf

Probate • The process by which a will is proved to the proper authorities (usually a probate court) to be valid

Publication • The act of giving some type of notice to the public—usually through a newspaper ad—of a petitioner's request for legal action (such as a change of name)

Real-estate agent • A middleman, generally representing the seller, who sells property and receives a commission based on the selling price

Real property • Land, including buildings and any interest in them (such as a lease or condominium ownership)

Residence requirements • State laws that prohibit persons from bringing certain suits (such as divorce) until one of the parties has lived in the state for a specified minimum period of time

Respondeat superior • A legal doctrine which holds one person (often an employer) legally responsible for wrongs committed by another (typically an employee) when the agent is acting on behalf of the other person

Respondent • The defendant in a lawsuit

Restrictive covenant • In real estate, an agreement binding subsequent owners of property to do or refrain from doing certain things (for example, building a wall that shades another's house)

Revolving credit account • An open-ended credit account in which a monthly payment must be made on the balance but other items may still be bought on the account, up to a certain limit

Secured debt • A debt whose payment is guaranteed by some other property (collateral) in the event of a default

Security deposit • Money required by a landlord to be paid by a tenant at the beginning of a lease and to be returned to the tenant at the end of the leasing arrangement if the premises are undamaged and no back rent is due

Separate maintenance • A "legal separation" arrangement whereby married parties live apart, free from harassment or control of one another, although they are not legally divorced

Separation agreement • A contract signed by husband and wife in contemplation of a separation or divorce, regarding such subjects as division of property, support, and custody of children

Service of process • The act of notifying all involved parties of legal proceedings about to take place

Settlement • In real estate, when a buyer and seller make final the sales process; the date when the buyer makes the remainder of his payment, and the seller signs the deed of title

Settlement sheet • A paper which sets out the costs (taxes, stamps, etc.) to be paid by the seller and the buyer and the amount paid to each of them and to others (such as the real-estate broker, title company, attorney, etc.)

Sole proprietorship • A form of business where the owner acts alone and is personally responsible for all debts and losses incurred by the business

Statute of limitations • A law which prohibits a claimant from bringing a lawsuit after a specified number of years have passed from the date of the claimed injury

Sublease • The renting of an unexpired lease by an original tenant to a third party; it neither terminates the original tenant's obligation to pay rent to the landlord nor creates a direct landlord-tenant relationship between the landlord and the third-party tenant

Subpoena • A court order requiring a witness to appear at the time the case is heard, and/or requiring that certain records be brought forth

Tenancy at sufferance • A type of informal tenancy when there is no valid written lease and either landlord or tenant can end their relationship at any time without notice

Tenancy at will • A written rental agreement which continues until either the landlord or the tenant gives proper notice to the other of an intention to end the lease

Tenancy by the entirety • A form of joint ownership allowed only to married couples; similar to a joint tenancy except that neither spouse can sell his or her share without permission of the other, and the tenancy can be terminated only by death, divorce, or mutual agreement

Tenancy for years • A long-term written lease which provides that the tenancy expires on a specific date in the future, without the need for either landlord or tenant to act or give notice

Tenant • A person who rents premises from another (the landlord)

Testator • One who makes a will

Title insurance • An insurance policy that protects either the owner or lender or both against any legal defects in the title to a house (such as unreleased mortgages or liens on the property that the buyer or seller did not know about)

Trust • A legal arrangement where ownership of certain property or funds is given to a trustee, who must act for the benefit of another person (the beneficiary) as directed by the document creating the trust

Unsecured debt • A debt whose payment is not backed up by specific property in the event of a default

Usury • The charging of an unlawfully high rate of interest when lending money

Venue • The particular county or city in which a court with jurisdiction may hear and decide a case

Verification • A signed statement in which a petitioner swears the facts contained in his petition are true, and that if necessary the petitioner is prepared to testify to them under oath or to prove them through documentation

Warranty • A promise that the manufacturer or seller of an item makes about his product; may be either *express* (stated in writing or verbally) or *implied* (found to exist automatically, by virtue of the type of product involved)

Will • A legal document in which a person states what he wishes to happen to his property upon his death

Appendix I

GROUNDS FOR DIVORCE, BY STATE

JUST as marriage itself must conform to certain legal requirements in order to be valid, a divorce or dissolution of marriage must also follow certain rules. Because each state has its own grounds and because laws are subject to change, you should check with the divorce court's clerk before proceeding.

Residency refers to the length of time required from the time the divorce petition is filed, unless otherwise indicated. *Remarriage* refers to the period beginning with the effective date of the decree.

Laws vary from state to state and change from year to year. Consult your local library for the latest statutory revisions. As of January 1981, grounds available for divorce in each state (and residency and remarriage requirements) were as follows:

Alabama

1. Abandonment for more than one year
2. Adultery
3. Crime against nature before or after marriage
4. Cruelty or any cause justifying divorce, if plaintiff desires separation only (also known as a partial divorce)
5. Final decree of partial divorce in effect for more than two years
6. Five successive years in insane asylum after marriage, the person so confined being hopelessly and incurably insane when divorce is filed
7. Habitual drunkenness or drug addiction contracted after marriage

8. Imprisonment in penitentiary for two years under sentence of seven years or more
9. Incapacity
10. Incompatibility
11. Nonsupport of wife by husband for two years will permit wife to obtain divorce
12. Physical violence
13. Pregnancy of wife at time of marriage without husband's knowledge will permit husband to obtain divorce
14. Irretrievable breakdown of marriage

Residency: Six months
Remarriage: Sixty days

Alaska

1. Adultery
2. Conviction of a felony
3. Cruelty impairing health or endangering life or personal indignities rendering life burdensome
4. Failure to consummate at time of marriage and continuing until commencement of legal action
5. Habitual and gross drunkenness, begun after marriage and continuing for one year
6. Habitual addiction to drugs after marriage
7. Incompatibility of temperament
8. Incurable mental illness if spouse is confined to an institution for at least eighteen months prior to the filing of the divorce
9. Willful desertion for one year
10. Willful neglect by the husband to provide necessaries of life for the wife for twelve months, when failure is because of his idleness, profligacy, or dissipation

Residency: None
Remarriage: No restriction

Arizona

Court will enter decree of dissolution of marriage if residency requirement is met, conciliation provisions either do not apply or have been met, marriage is irretrievably broken, and, to the extent it has jurisdiction, court has considered and provided for child custody and support, spousal maintenance, and property disposition

Residency: Ninety days
Remarriage: No restriction

Arkansas

1. Adultery
2. Conviction of felony or infamous crime
3. Cruel and barbarous treatment endangering life of innocent party
4. Desertion for one year without reasonable cause
5. Habitual drunkenness for one year
6. Indignities to person of innocent party
7. Insanity—continuous confinement to institution for three years or adjudicated insane more than three years before filing of suit
8. Impotency at time of marriage continuing to time of bringing action for divorce
9. Parties have lived apart for three consecutive years without cohabitation
10. Spouse by former undissolved marriage living at time of marriage
11. Willful nonsupport

Residency: Sixty days preceding commencement of action
Remarriage: No restriction

California

1. Incurable insanity, requiring proof by competent medical or psychiatric testimony
2. Irreconcilable differences which have caused irremediable breakdown of marriage

Residency: Six months
Remarriage: No restriction

Colorado

Irretrievable breakdown of marriage relationship must be proved as essential element of action

Residency: Ninety days
Remarriage: No restriction

Connecticut

1. Adultery
2. Fraudulent contract
3. Habitual intemperance
4. Incompatibility causing parties to live apart for continuous period of at least eighteen months with no reasonable prospect of reconciliation
5. Infamous crime involving a violation of conjugal duty and punishable by imprisonment for more than a year
6. Intolerable cruelty
7. Irretrievable breakdown of marriage
8. Mental illness causing legal confinement for an accumulated period of at least five years within the six-year period next preceding complaint
9. Sentence to imprisonment for life
10. Seven years' absence, unheard from
11. Willful desertion for a year

Residency: One year
Remarriage: No restriction

Delaware

1. Separation caused by incompatibility
2. Separation caused by respondent's mental illness
3. Separation caused by respondent's misconduct, including adultery, bigamy, conviction of a serious crime, physical or oral abuse, desertion, homosexuality, refusal to perform marriage obligations, contracting venereal disease, habitual alcoholism or drug abuse

Residency: Six months
Remarriage: No restriction

District of Columbia

1. Parties living separately for one year
2. Parties living separately voluntarily for six months

Residency: Six months
Remarriage: No restriction

Florida

1. Marriage irretrievably broken
2. Mental incompetence of a party for three years

Residency: Six months
Remarriage: No restriction

Georgia

1. Adultery
2. Conviction of offense involving moral turpitude with penalty of two years or more in penitentiary
3. Cruel treatment, consisting of willful infliction of pain, bodily or mental, upon complaining party, such as reasonably justifies apprehension of danger to life, limb, or health
4. Force, menaces, duress, or fraud in obtaining marriage
5. Habitual intoxication
6. Habitual addiction to drugs
7. Impotency at time of marriage
8. Incurable mental illness for two years
9. Irretrievably broken marriage
10. Mental incapacity at time of marriage
11. Pregnancy at time of marriage, unknown by husband
12. Relationship between parties such that marriage is prohibited
13. Willful and continued desertion for one year

Residency: Six months
Remarriage: Judge or jury determines rights and disabilities of parties

Hawaii

1. Expiration of term in decree of separate bed and board without reconciliation
2. Living separate and apart for two years or more
3. Marriage irretrievably broken

4. Satisfaction of court that divorce would not be harsh, oppressive, or contrary to public interest

Residency: Six months
Remarriage: No restriction (if wife remarries, alimony must be modified)

Idaho

1. Adultery
2. Conviction of a felony
3. Extreme cruelty
4. Habitual intemperance
5. Irreconcilable differences determined by court to be substantial reasons to dissolve marriage
6. Living separate and apart five years
7. Willful desertion
8. Willful neglect

Residency: Six weeks
Remarriage: No restriction

Illinois

1. Adultery
2. Another husband or wife at time of marriage
3. Attempt on life of spouse by poisoning or other means showing malice
4. Conviction of a felony or infamous crime
5. Desertion for one year
6. Excessive use of addictive drugs for two years
7. Extreme and repeated mental or physical cruelty
8. Habitual drunkenness for two years
9. Impotency
10. Infection of spouse with venereal disease

Residency: Ninety days
Remarriage: No restriction

Indiana

1. Conviction of infamous crime
2. Impotency at time of marriage
3. Incurable insanity for two years
4. Irretrievable breakdown of marriage

Residency: Six months and, in county filed, three months
Remarriage: Verified application. No license issued to male with dependent children from prior marriages reasonably dependent on him for support, unless person provides proof with his application he is supporting or contributing to support his children by prior marriages and complying with court support orders.

Iowa

Breakdown of marriage in that legitimate objects of matrimony have been destroyed and no reasonable likelihood that relationship can be preserved

Residency: One year
Remarriage: No restriction

Kansas

1. Abandonment for one year
2. Adultery
3. Confinement in an institution for mental illness or adjudication of mental illness by court without restoration therefrom and without confinement for more than three years; and in either case, a finding by two of three court-appointed physicians that defendant has poor prognosis for recovery from such illness
4. Conviction of a felony and imprisonment therefor subsequent to the marriage
5. Extreme cruelty
6. Gross neglect of duty
7. Habitual drunkenness
8. Incompatibility

Residency: Sixty days
Remarriage: Parties cannot remarry until thirty days after entry of

divorce decree, unless an appeal is taken (and then not until receipt of mandate from appellate court)

Kentucky

Irretrievable breakdown of marriage is sole basis for dissolution.

Residency: One of the parties must have been maintained in the state for 180 days before the filing of the petition, must be proved by testimony of one or more witnesses
Remarriage: No restriction

Louisiana

Separation from bed and board may be claimed for

1. Abandonment
2. Adultery
3. Attempt on the life of the other
4. Conviction of a felony and sentence to death or to imprisonment at hard labor
5. Habitual intemperance, excesses, cruel treatment, or outrages if such conduct is of such a nature as to render living together insupportable
6. Having been charged with a felony and having fled from justice
7. Intentional nonsupport
8. Public defamation
9. Voluntary living separate and apart for one year without reconciliation

Separation may be allowed when spouses have lived six months separate and apart voluntarily and they execute affidavit to that effect, including statement of existence of irreconcilable differences to such degree and nature as to render their living together insupportable and impossible. Divorce may be granted immediately for one of the following causes:

1. Adultery
2. Conviction of a felony and sentence of death or imprisonment at hard labor

Divorce on any of the other grounds may not be granted unless separation from bed and board has been decreed and one year has elapsed thereafter without reconciliation. When married persons have been living separate and apart for two or more years, either party may sue for absolute divorce.

Residency: None, except as stated above
Remarriage: No restriction

Maine

1. Adultery
2. Cruel and abusive treatment
3. Extreme cruelty
4. Gross and confirmed habits of intoxication from use of intoxicating liquors or drugs
5. Impotence
6. Irreconcilable differences
7. Nonsupport
8. Utter desertion continued for three consecutive years

Residency: Parties must have been married here or cohabited here after marriage, or plaintiff must have resided here when cause of action occurred, or plaintiff must reside here in good faith for six months before action is begun, or defendant must be resident of the state
Remarriage: No restriction

Maryland

1. Abandonment for twelve months without reasonable expectation of reconciliation
2. Adultery
3. Any cause rendering marriage null and void from the beginning under Maryland law
4. Conviction of a felony or misdemeanor and sentence of at least three years or indeterminate sentence in penal institution, twelve months of which have been served
5. Impotency
6. Permanent and incurable insanity
7. Voluntary separation without cohabitation for twelve consecutive months without reasonable expectation of reconciliation

8. Statutory separation (for period of three years)
(Cruelty can serve as basis for legal separation)

Residency: One year. Insanity, two years
Remarriage: No restriction

Massachusetts

1. Adultery
2. Cruel and abusive treatment
3. Gross and confirmed habits of intoxication caused by voluntary, excessive use of liquor or drugs
4. Gross and cruel failure to support
5. Impotency
6. Irretrievable breakdown of marriage
7. Sentence to confinement for life or five years in penal or reformatory institution
8. Utter desertion for one year

Residency: Plaintiff must live in commonwealth for one year, and cause must have occurred within commonwealth
Remarriage: Allowed after divorce judgment becomes absolute (i.e., after six months); if spouse remarries after seven years of mate's absence, not guilty of polygamy

Michigan

Breakdown of marriage relationship to extent that objects of matrimony have been destroyed and there remains no reasonable likelihood that marriage can be preserved

Residency: Plaintiff must have lived in state 180 days unless marriage was solemnized in state and plaintiff lived in state from marriage to bringing suit.

One spouse must have resided in county ten days before bringing suit.

If not voluntary appearance, defendant must live in state when divorce filed or when cause arose, unless brought in by publication or personally served with process within state or personally served with order for appearance and publication anywhere.

When cause happened outside Michigan, one party must live in state for one year.
Remarriage: No restriction

Minnesota

Irretrievable breakdown of marriage—defenses abolished

Residency: One party must live in state 180 days
Remarriage: No provisions

Mississippi

1. Adultery, unless collusion or condonation
2. Consanguinity within prohibited degrees
3. Habitual cruel and inhuman treatment
4. Habitual excessive use of drugs
5. Incurable insanity, if insane party has been under treatment and confined to institution for three years
6. Insanity or idiocy at time of marriage, unknown to complaining party
7. Irreconcilable differences if not contested and if provisions are made for custody after sixty days
8. Pregnancy by other than husband
9. Prior marriage undissolved
10. Natural impotency
11. Sentence to penitentiary, unless pardoned

Residency: One party must live in state for six months unless residence acquired to secure divorce
Remarriage: In case of adultery, court may prohibit remarriage; such prohibition may be removed by court after one year, for good cause shown

Missouri

Irreconcilably broken marriage with no reasonable likelihood it can be preserved

Residency: Ninety days
Remarriage: No restriction

Montana

Irretrievable breakdown of marriage supported by

1. Not having lived together for 180 days
2. Serious marital discord adversely affecting one of the parties

Residency: Ninety days
Remarriage: No restriction except during appeal challenging finding that marriage was irretrievably broken

Nebraska

Marriage irretrievably broken

Residency: One party for one year with bona fide intent of making state his home, or married in state and one party has stayed there since marriage
Remarriage: No restriction

Nevada

1. Incompatibility
2. Insanity for two years
3. No cohabitation for one year

Residency: Six weeks
Remarriage: No restriction

New Hampshire

1. Abandonment and refusal to cohabit for two years
2. Adultery
3. Disappearance for two years
4. Desertion for two years
5. Extreme cruelty
6. Habitual drunkenness for two years
7. Impotency
8. Imprisonment for more than one year
9. Irreconcilable differences leading to irretrievable breakdown of marriage

10. Joining any religious sect or society forbidding cohabitation of husband and wife and six months' refusal to cohabit
11. Treatment such as to seriously injure health or seriously endanger reason

Residency: One year; jurisdiction only when cause of divorce arose while plaintiff was living in state
Remarriage: No restriction

New Jersey

1. Adultery
2. Deviate sexual conduct voluntarily performed by defendant without consent of plaintff
3. Desertion for one year or more
4. Extreme cruelty for three months before filing
5. Imprisonment for eighteen months, provided that, if imprisonment ended before filing, couple did not resume cohabitation
6. Institutionalization for mental illness for two years or more after marriage
7. Separation for eighteen consecutive months, if no reasonable prospect of reconciliation
8. Voluntarily induced addiction or habituation to narcotic drug or habitual drunkenness for twelve months after marriage

Residency: Either party bona fide resident of state and has stayed such, except that no divorce can be commenced on grounds other than adultery unless one of the parties has lived in state for one year
Remarriage: No restriction

New Mexico

1. Abandonment
2. Adultery
3. Cruel or inhuman treatment
4. Incompatibility

Residency: Six months
Remarriage: No restriction

New York

1. Abandonment for one year
2. Adultery
3. Cruel or inhuman treatment
4. Imprisonment of defendant for three years after marriage
5. Living apart for one year

Residency: Parties married in state and lived there for one year; parties lived in state as husband and wife for one year; cause occurred in state and either party lived there for one year; cause occurred in state and both parties lived there when action commenced; either party lived in state two years before action commenced
Remarriage: No restriction

North Carolina

1. Adultery
2. Bestiality
3. Crime against nature
4. Impotency at time of marriage and continuing
5. Incurable insanity causing separation for three years
6. Pregnancy of wife by another at time of marriage without knowledge of husband
7. Separation for one year

Residency: Six months
Remarriage: No restriction

North Dakota

1. Adultery
2. Conviction of a felony
3. Extreme cruelty
4. Habitual intemperance for one year
5. Insanity with five years' confinement in an institution
6. Irreconcilable differences
7. Willful desertion for one year
8. Willful neglect for one year

Residency: Twelve months for plaintiff if a citizen of the United States or has declared intent to become one; for insanity, complainant must have lived in state five years
Remarriage: Must be specifically permitted by court

Ohio

1. Adultery
2. Extreme cruelty
3. Fraudulent contract
4. Gross neglect of duty
5. Habitual drunkenness
6. Imprisonment in penitentiary
7. Impotency
8. Lived apart for two years
9. Lived apart for four years if one party in mental institution
10. Other spouse living at time of marriage to this spouse
11. Procurement of divorce outside of state by spouse
12. Willful absence for one year

Residency: Six months for plaintiff
Remarriage: No restriction

Oklahoma

1. Abandonment for one year
2. Adultery
3. Extreme cruelty
4. Fraudulent contract
5. Gross neglect of duty
6. Habitual drunkenness
7. Impotency
8. Imprisonment for felony at time action was filed
9. Insanity for five years
10. Pregnancy of wife at time of marriage by one other than husband
11. Procurement of divorce by spouse in other state
12. Incompatibility

Residency: Six months in good faith, thirty days in county of residence; five years for grounds of insanity
Remarriage: Six months after divorce decree

Oregon

1. Either party lacked legal age or sufficient understanding and has not been sufficiently notified
2. Irreconcilable differences
3. Marriage procured by force or fraud

Residency: None if married in state, otherwise six months
Remarriage: Provisions ambiguous—check with attorney

Pennsylvania

1. Adultery
2. Conviction of certain crimes resulting in two or more years sentence
3. Consanguinity or affinity
4. Cruel and barbarous treatment
5. Desertion for two years
6. Endangering life
7. Existing prior marriage
8. Incompatibility
9. Indignities suffered rendering condition intolerable and life burdensome
10. Insanity or serious mental disorder
11. Uncondoned fraud, force, or coercion

Residency: Six months
Remarriage: Either may remarry, but defendant guilty of adultery may not marry other party to adultery during life of plaintiff

Puerto Rico

1. Abandonment for over one year
2. Absolute incurable impotency occurring after marriage
3. Adultery
4. Attempt to corrupt son or prostitute daughter and commerce in such corruption or prostitution

5. Conviction of a felony which may involve loss of civil rights
6. Cruel treatment or grave injury
7. Habitual drunkenness or excessive use of drugs
8. Incurable insanity if it seriously prevents spouses living together spiritually
9. Proposal of husband to prostitute wife
10. Separation for two years

Residency: One year, unless ground arose in Puerto Rico or while one spouse lived there
Remarriage: Not prohibited, but if woman remarries within 301 days of divorce, she must provide certification as to whether or not she is pregnant, for purposes of establishing paternity.

Rhode Island

1. Adultery
2. Any other gross misbehavior or wickedness repugnant to and in violation of marriage covenant
3. Continued drunkenness
4. Extreme cruelty
5. Habitual, excessive intemperate use of narcotics
6. Impotency
7. Irreconcilable differences
8. Marriage originally void or voidable by law
9. Neglect or refusal for one year of husband to provide for subsistence of wife if he is of sufficient ability
10. Party deemed to be, or treated as if, civilly dead, for crime committed
11. Separation for three years
12. Willful desertion for five years

Residency: One year for either party; or in case of divorce from bed, board, and future cohabitation (not just from bond of marriage), must have resided in state for such time as court deems sufficient
Remarriage: No restriction

South Carolina

1. Adultery
2. Continuous separation for one year

3. Desertion for one year
4. Habitual drunkenness caused by alcohol or narcotics
5. Physical cruelty

Residency: One year; if both parties are residents, three months
Remarriage: No restriction

South Dakota

1. Adultery
2. Extreme cruelty
3. Willful desertion
4. Willful negligence
5. Habitual intemperance
6. Conviction of felony
7. Incurable, chronic mania or dementia of either spouse five years or more while under confinement by order of court or appropriate agency

Residency: One party must live in state; sixty days mandatory "cooling off" period following institution of suit
Remarriage: No restriction

Tennessee

1. Adultery
2. Attempts on life of other by means showing malice
3. Bigamy
4. Conviction of an infamous crime
5. Conviction of a felony
6. Desertion for one year without reasonable cause
7. Habitual drunkenness or drug abuse
8. Impotence
9. Irreconcilable differences
10. Refusal of wife to move to Tennessee and absence from husband for two years
11. Wife pregnant at time of marriage with another man's child without knowledge of husband

Residency: No requirements if plaintiff lived in state when acts were committed; if one or other lived in state six months before filing, complaint can be filed on acts committed elsewhere
Remarriage: No restriction

Texas

1. Abandonment for one year
2. Adultery
3. Cruel treatment which makes living together insupportable
4. Discord or conflict of personalities that destroys legitimate ends of marriage and prevents reasonable expectation of reconciliation
5. Felony conviction and imprisonment if twelve months after final judgment (and not if pardoned or convicted on spouse's testimony)
6. Living apart for three years
7. Mental illness with three-year hospitalization without hope for permanent recovery

Residency: Six months in state, ninety days in county
Remarriage: No restriction after thirty days

Utah

1. Adultery
2. Desertion for one year
3. Felony conviction
4. Habitual drunkenness
5. Impotency at time of marriage
6. Permanent insanity
7. Physical or mental cruelty
8. Separation for three years
9. Willful neglect to provide common necessities of life

Residency: Three months in state and county
Remarriage: Prohibited during appeal or period allowed for appeal

Vermont

1. Adultery
2. Failure to provide suitable maintenance if able to do so

3. Insanity commitment for five years
4. Intolerable severity
5. Prison confinement
6. Separation for six months with resumption of marital relations not reasonably probable
7. Willful desertion or absence for seven years

Residency: Six months; two years for insanity
Remarriage: No restriction

Virginia

1. Adultery
2. Cruelty, after one-year separation for it
3. Desertion for one year
4. Felony conviction for one year
5. Separation for one year without cohabitation
6. Sodomy or buggery outside marriage

Numbers 1 and 6 not valid if parties voluntarily cohabited after knowledge of such act; if it happened five years earlier; or if it was committed by procurement or connivance of party alleging it

Residency: Six months
Remarriage: Allowed after appeals

Virgin Islands

Breakdown of marriage relationship without likelihood that marriage can be preserved

Residency: Six weeks
Remarriage: No restriction

Washington

1. Marriage irretrievably broken
2. Marriage invalid—grounds for invalidity:
   a. Consanguinity
   b. Mental incapacity

    c. Lack of capacity to consent; or consent obtained by force, duress, or fraud

    d. Lack of parental or court approval

    e. Nonvoluntary cohabitation after attaining age of consent after cessation of force or duress or discovery of fraud

    f. Prior undissolved marriage

Residency: No specific duration
Remarriage: No restriction, except during appeal of finding that marriage is irretrievably broken

West Virginia

1. Abandonment for six months
2. Adultery
3. Child abuse or neglect
4. Cruel and unreasonable treatment or fear of bodily hurt
5. Drug addiction
6. Felony conviction
7. Habitual drunkenness
8. Insanity
9. Irreconcilable differences (sixty-day waiting period required)
10. Separation for one year

Residency: One year
Remarriage: No restriction

Wisconsin

Irretrievably broken marriage, marriage being irretrievably broken if

1. Both parties so state
2. One party so states, and one-year separation
3. One party so states and judge finds no possibility of reconciliation
4. One party so states and, after judge finds marriage not irretrievably broken, either party states under oath that it is irretrievably broken

Residency: Six months in state, thirty days in county
Remarriage: Six months' waiting period

Wyoming

1. Insanity confinement for two years
2. Irreconcilable differences

Residency: Plaintiff must reside in state for sixty days
Remarriage: No restriction

Appendix II

SAMPLE POWERS OF ATTORNEY

Sample Power of Attorney (General)

KNOW ALL PERSONS BY THESE PRESENTS:

I, Mark Jones, of 1 North Two Street, Baltimore, Maryland, do hereby constitute and appoint Susan Smith of 2 North Two Street, Baltimore, Maryland, as my true sufficient and lawful attorney in fact, to act in, manage and conduct all my estate, affairs, undertakings and business, and for that purpose in my name, place and stead and on my behalf, to do and execute any or all of the following acts, deeds and things as fully and in every respect as I might or could do were I personally present at the doing thereof:

[LIST SOME EXPLICIT POWERS]

And I hereby declare that any act or thing done hereunder by my said attorney shall be binding on myself, and my heirs, legal and personal representatives and assigns, whether the same shall have been done before or after my death, or other revocation of this instrument, unless and until reliable intelligence or notice of my death shall have been received by my said attorney, or until a revocation of this instrument has been received by my said attorney.

This Power of Attorney shall not be affected upon my disability, incompetence or inability to act and in such event, I hereby nominate and appoint my herein named attorney as my legal guardian and release him/her from posting bond as such.

IN WITNESS WHEREOF I have hereunto executed and sealed this power this _____ day of _____, in the year 19____.

WITNESS:

_____   _____(SEAL)

(Name of Grantor)

WITNESS:

_____

STATE OF MARYLAND, CITY OF BALTIMORE, to wit:

I, _____, do hereby certify that I am a duly commissioned, qualified, and authorized Notary Public in and for _____, State of Maryland, and grantor in the foregoing Power of Attorney, dated the _____ day of _____, 19____, and hereto annexed, who is known to me as the person who executed the foregoing Power of Attorney, appeared before me this day within the territorial limits of my authority, and being first duly sworn, executed said instrument after the contents thereof had been read and duly explained to him and acknowledged that the execution of said instrument by him was his free and voluntary act and deed for the uses and purposes therein set forth.

IN WITNESS WHEREOF, I have hereunto set my hand and affixed my Notarial Seal this _____ day of _____, 19____.

_____

Notary Public

My Commission Expires:

_____

Sample Power of Attorney (Specific)

KNOW ALL PERSONS BY THESE PRESENTS, That I,
_____, appoint _____
attorney for me and in my stead with the following powers:
[INCLUDE ONLY THE POWERS APPLICABLE]

    1) ____ may prosecute or defend all law suits or actions in my name which concern any real or personal property I now own or will own.

    2) ____ may deposit any money received in a bank in my name: ____ may withdraw and deposit such items for my benefit as ____ sees fit.

    4) ____ may receive and perform for me and, in my stead, sign and endorse checks, including Social Security or any type of medical benefit checks, and execute any and all instruments.

    5) ____ may act in relation to my estate, real and personal, as fully and in all respects, as I myself could do.

THIS POWER OF ATTORNEY becomes effective upon a satisfactory showing that I lack sufficient understanding or capacity to make or communicate responsible decisions concerning myself, including provisions for health care, food, clothing, or shelter, because of any mental disability, senility, other mental weakness, or disease or accident.

THIS POWER OF ATTORNEY continues only so long as I remain incapacitated for any of the above-mentioned reasons, and terminates upon the determination that I am no longer disabled.

IN WITNESS AND ACKNOWLEDGMENT THEREOF, I hereunto set my hand and seal this ____ day of _____, in the year one thousand nine hundred and _____.

                                          _____(SEAL)

STATE OF MARYLAND, CITY OF BALTIMORE, TO WIT:

I HEREBY CERTIFY, That on this ____ day of _____, 19 ____, before me, the subscriber, a Notary Public of the State of Maryland, in and for Baltimore City, personally appeared _____

_____, known to me or satisfactorily proven to be the person whose name is subscribed to the within instrument, and acknowledged that _____ executed the same for the purpose therein contained, and in my presence signed and sealed the same.

IN WITNESS WHEREOF, I hereunto set my hand and official seal.

_____

NOTARY PUBLIC

My Commission Expires:

_____

Appendix III

AGENCIES FOR INCORPORATING, BY STATE

IN most jurisdictions, corporate charters and related papers must be filed with the secretary of state or other state officer. Except in Idaho and Pennsylvania, this officer is also empowered to receive service of process against a corporation chartered in the state. A list of the appropriate officers follows:

State	Filing
Alabama	Secretary of State Montgomery, Alabama 36100
Alaska	Commissioner of Commerce Juneau, Alaska 99801
Arizona	Corporation Commission Phoenix, Arizona 85000
Arkansas	Secretary of State Little Rock, Arkansas 72200
California	Secretary of State Sacramento, California 95801
Colorado	Secretary of State Denver, Colorado 80200
Connecticut	Secretary of State Hartford, Connecticut 06100

Source: IBP Research & Editorial Staff, *The Lawyer's Desk Book*, 7th Ed. (Englewood Cliffs, N.J.: Institute for Business Planning, Inc., 1981).

Delaware	Secretary of State Dover, Delaware 19901
District of Columbia	Office of Supt. of Corporations Washington, D.C. 20001
Florida	Secretary of State Tallahassee, Florida 32301
Georgia	Secretary of State Atlanta, Georgia 30300
Hawaii	Director of Regulation Agencies P.O. Box 40 Honolulu, Hawaii 96810
Idaho*	Secretary of State Boise, Idaho 83700
Illinois	Secretary of State Springfield, Illinois 62700
Indiana	Secretary of State Indianapolis, Indiana 46200
Iowa	Secretary of State Des Moines, Iowa 50300
Kansas	Secretary of State Topeka, Kansas 66600
Kentucky	Secretary of State Frankfort, Kentucky 40601
Louisiana	Secretary of State Baton Rouge, Louisiana 70800
Maine	Secretary of State Augusta, Maine 04301
Maryland	State Dept. of Assessment and Taxation Baltimore, Maryland, 21200
Massachusetts	Secretary of the Commonwealth Boston, Massachusetts 02100
Michigan	Department of Commerce Corporation Division P.O. Drawer C Lansing, Michigan 48904

*Service of process is made upon the county auditor.

Minnesota	Secretary of State St. Paul, Minnesota 55100
Mississippi	Secretary of State Jackson, Mississippi 39200
Missouri	Secretary of State Jefferson City, Missouri 65101
Montana	Secretary of State Helena, Montana 59601
Nebraska	Secretary of State Lincoln, Nebraska 68500
Nevada	Secretary of State Carson City, Nevada 89701
New Hampshire	Secretary of State Concord, New Hampshire 03300
New Jersey	Secretary of State Trenton, New Jersey 08600
New Mexico	State Corporation Commission Santa Fe, New Mexico 87501
New York	Secretary of State Albany, New York 12200
North Carolina	Secretary of State Raleigh, North Carolina 27600
North Dakota	Secretary of State Bismarck, North Dakota 58501
Ohio	Secretary of State Columbus, Ohio 43200
Oklahoma	Secretary of State Oklahoma City, Oklahoma 73100
Oregon	Corporation Commissioner Salem, Oregon 97301
Pennsylvania*	Department of State Harrisburg, Pennsylvania 17101

*Service of process is made upon the Secretary of the Commonwealth, Harrisburg, Pa. 17101

Puerto Rico

Secretary of State
P.O. Box 3271
San Juan, Puerto Rico 00904

Rhode Island

Secretary of State
Providence, Rhode Island 02900

South Carolina

Secretary of State
Columbia, South Carolina 29200

South Dakota

Secretary of State
Pierre, South Dakota 57501

Tennessee

Secretary of State
Nashville, Tennessee 37200

Texas

Secretary of State
Austin, Texas 78700

Utah

Secretary of State
Salt Lake City, Utah 84100

Vermont

Secretary of State
Montpelier, Vermont 05601

Virginia

State Corporation Commission
Richmond, Virginia 23200

Washington

Secretary of State
Olympia, Washington 98501

West Virginia

Secretary of State
Charleston, West Virginia 25300

Wisconsin

Secretary of State
Madison, Wisconsin 53700

Wyoming

Secretary of State
Cheyenne, Wyoming 82001

Appendix IV

SMALL-CLAIMS COURTS,
BY STATE

NOTE: Legislation is pending in several states to raise the amount for which you can sue, as well as other aspects of the small-claims system. Check with your local clerk for the currency and accuracy of the following data.

Alabama

Name of court: District Court, located in each county; listed under name of county or state

Venue: The respondent must reside or do business within the jurisdiction of the court

Claim limit: $500

Alaska

Name of court: District Court; listed under state of Alaska, District Court, Small Claims

Venue: The respondent must reside within the jurisdiction of the court

Claim limit: $2,000

Arizona

Name of court: County Court, Small Claims Part, justice of the peace; listed under name of county; in some rural areas, listed under name of local community, Justice Court

Venue: The respondent must reside within the jurisdiction of the court

Claim limit: $2,500

Arkansas	Name of court: County Court or Municipal Court; listed under name of county
	Venue: Either the respondent must reside within the jurisdiction of the court, or the action must have taken place within the jurisdiction of the court
	Claim limit: Property damage, $100; other claims, $300
California	Name of court: Municipal Court; listed under name of local government or county, Municipal or Justice Court
	Venue: Either the respondent must reside within the jurisdiction of the court, or the action must have taken place within the jurisdiction of the court
	Claim limit: $750 ($1,500 in jurisdiction of San Bernardino [Chino Division], East Los Angeles, West Orange County, Fresno, Compton and Oakland-Piedmont)
	Note: Lawyers are not allowed
Colorado	Name of court: County Court, Small Claims Division; listed under name of county
	Venue: The respondent must either reside within the jurisdiction of the court, or do business within the jurisdiction of the court
	Claim limit: $500 (legislation pending to raise limit to $1,000)
	Note: The respondent may bring an attorney only if the claimant has brought an attorney
Connecticut	Name of court: Superior Court, twenty-one geographic districts statewide; listed under state of Connecticut, Superior Court
	Venue: The respondent must reside within the jurisdiction of the court
	Claim limit: $750
Delaware	Name of court: Justice of the Peace Court; listed under state of Delaware

Venue: Action must have occurred within
the jurisdiction of the court
Claim limit: $1,500

District of Columbia   Name of court: District Court; listed under
District of Columbia
Venue: Either the respondent must reside
within the jurisdiction of the court, or the
action must have occurred within the jurisdiction of the court
Claim limit: $750

Florida   Name of court: County Court, Civil Division; listed under name of county
Venue: Either the respondent must reside
or do business within the jurisdiction of
the court, or the action must have occurred within the jurisdiction of the court
Claim limit: $1,500

Georgia   Name of court: State Court, Small Claims
Division in large cities; Justice of the
Peace Court in rural counties
Venue: The respondent must reside within
the jurisdiction of the court
Claim limit: Large cities, $299.99; rural
areas (Justice of the Peace Courts), $200

Hawaii   Name of court: District Court; listed under
state of Hawaii, Judiciary Department
Venue: The respondent must reside or do
business within the jurisdiction of the
court
Claim limit: $1,000
Note: Lawyers are not allowed for security
deposit cases

Idaho   Name of court: County Court within judicial
district; listed under name of county,
Magistrate Division, county district
Venue: The respondent must reside or do
business within the jurisdiction of the
court

Claim limit: $1,000

Note: Lawyers are not allowed

Illinois

Name of court: In Chicago, Municipal District Court; listed under city of Chicago, otherwise, County Court; listed under name of county

Venue: Either the respondent must reside within the jurisdiction of the court, or the action must have taken place within the jurisdiction of the court

Claim limit: Chicago, $1,000; under $500, the plaintiff must not be represented by an attorney; for claims between $500 and $1,000, either side may be represented by an attorney; outlying areas, $2,500

Indiana

Name of court: County Court, Small Claims Division; Justice Courts in rural counties, listed under name of county

Venue: Either the respondent must reside within the jurisdiction of the court, or the action must have taken place within the jurisdiction of the court

Claim limit: $1,500

Iowa

Name of court: District Court; listed under state of Iowa, District Court, Small Claims Division

Venue: Action must have occurred within the jurisdiction of the court

Claim limit: $1,000

Kansas

Name of court: District Court, Limited Actions Division in certain areas; otherwise, District Court, listed under name of county

Venue: The respondent must reside within the jurisdiction of the court

Claim limit: $500

Kentucky

Name of court: District Court, Small Claims Division; listed under state of Kentucky, Government offices, Small Claims

Venue: The respondent must reside within the jurisdiction of the court
Claim limit: $1,000

Louisiana
Name of court: City Court or Parish Court; listed under Government section, City Court, Small Claims Division
Venue: The respondent must reside within the jurisdiction of the court
Claim limit: $750

Maine
Name of court: District Court; listed under state of Maine, District Court, Small Claims
Venue: Either the respondent must reside within the jurisdiction of the court, or the action must have occurred within the jurisdiction of the court
Claim limit: $800

Maryland
Name of court: District Court; listed under state of Maryland or county, Civil Division, Small Claims
Venue: Either the respondent must reside within the jurisdiction of the court, or the action must have occurred within the jurisdiction of the court
Claim limit: $500

Massachusetts
Name of court: Municipal Court in urban areas; otherwise, District Court statewide; listed under local government, Municipal Court, or state of Massachusetts, District Court
Venue: The respondent must reside within the jurisdiction of the court
Claim limit: Varies, but generally $750 (legislation is pending to raise the limit to $1,200)

Michigan
Name of court: District Court; listed under state of Michigan, District Court, Civil Division

Venue: The respondent must reside within the jurisdiction of the court

Claim limit: Detroit, $300; elsewhere, $600

Minnesota

Name of court: In Minneapolis, County Court, Municipal Division, Small Claims, listed under name of county; statewide, Municipal Court, listed under name of county

Claim limit: $1,000

Mississippi

Name of court: Justice Court; listed under local municipality or local justice of the peace

Venue: The respondent must reside within the jurisdiction of the court

Claim limit: $500

Missouri

Name of court: County Court; listed under name of county

Venue: Either the respondent must reside within the jurisdiction of the court, or the action must have occurred within the jurisdiction of the court

Claim limit: $500

Montana

Name of court: Justice of the Peace Court; listed under county government, Justice Court, or by contacting specific justice of the peace

Venue: The respondent must reside within the jurisdiction of the court or do business within the jurisdiction of the court

Claim limit: $750

Nebraska

Name of court: Municipal Court, County Court; listed under name of city or county

Venue: Action must have occurred within the jurisdiction of the court

Claim limit: $1,000

Nevada

Name of court: Justice Court; listed under name of state or county, Justice Court, Small Claims

Venue: The respondent must reside within
the jurisdiction of the court
Claim limit: $750

New Hampshire   Name of court: District Court; listed under
name of city
Venue: Either the respondent must reside
within the jurisdiction of the court, or
the action must have occurred within the
jurisdiction of the court
Claim limit: $500

New Jersey   Name of court: District Court, a division of
County Court; listed under name of
county
Venue: The respondent must reside within
the jurisdiction of the court
Claim limit: $500

New Mexico   Name of court: Metropolitan Court, Civil
Division; in outlying areas, may be Magistrates Court; listed under name of county
or state
Venue: Either the respondent must reside
within the jurisdiction of the court, or the
action must have occurred within the jurisdiction of the court
Claim limit: $5,000

New York   Name of court: City Court, Town Court,
Village Court, or District Court, depending on location; listed under local government
Venue: The respondent must reside or do
business within the jurisdiction of the
court
Claim limit: $1,500

North Carolina   Name of court: Superior Court, Small Claims
Division; listed under name of state
Venue: The respondent must reside within
the jurisdiction of the court
Claim limit: $800

North Dakota

Name of court: County Court, Small Claims Division; listed under name of county
Venue: The respondent must reside within the jurisdiction of the court
Claim limit: $1,000

Ohio

Name of court: Municipal County Court in cities; in other areas, County District Court; listed under name of city or county, Small Claims Division
Venue: The respondent must reside within the jurisdiction of the court
Claim limit: $500

Oklahoma

Name of court: County Court, Small Claims Division; listed under name of county
Venue: Either the respondent must reside within the jurisdiction of the court, or the action must have occurred within the jurisdiction of the court
Claim limit: $600

Oregon

Name of court: District Court or Justice Court, Small Claims Department; listed under name of county or local government
Venue: Action must have occurred within the jurisdiction of the court
Claim limit: $700
Note: Attorneys are not allowed

Pennsylvania

Name of court: In Philadelphia, Municipal Court, Small Claims Branch; in remainder of state, either County Court or Justice of the Peace Court; listed under local municipality or County Court, Small Claims Division
Venue: Either the respondent must reside within the jurisdiction of the court, or the action must have occurred within the jurisdiction of the court
Claim limit: Philadelphia, $1,000
Elsewhere, $2,000

Rhode Island	Name of court: State District Court; listed under name of state or county Venue: The respondent must reside within the jurisdiction of the court Claim limit: $500
South Carolina	Name of court: Magistrates Court; listed under County Government Venue: The respondent must reside within the jurisdiction of the court Claim limit: $1,000 (legislation is pending to raise the limit to $2,500)
South Dakota	Name of court: Circuit Court, Magistrates Division; listed under name of state or county, CirCourt, and also magistrate by name Venue: The respondent must reside within the jurisdiction of the court Claim limit: $2,000
Tennessee	Name of court: County Court, General Sessions Court; also may be Justice of the Peace Court; listed under name of county, General Sessions Court, Civil Division Venue: The respondent must reside within the jurisdiction of the court Claim limit: $2,000
Texas	Name of court: Justice of the Peace Court; listed under name of local municipality, Justice of the Peace Court, Small Claims Division Venue: The respondent must reside within the jurisdiction of the court Claim limit: $150 (legislation is pending to raise the limit); labor performed or wages, $200
Utah	Name of court: Circuit Court, Small Claims Division, listed under City Government, Circuit Court, or local municipality, Small Claims Division

Venue: Either the respondent must reside within the jurisdiction of the court, or the action must have occurred within the jurisdiction of the court

Claim limit: $400 (legislation is pending to raise the limit to $1,000)

Note: Lawyers are not allowed

Vermont

Name of court: District Court; listed under state of Vermont, District Court

Venue: The respondent must reside within the jurisdiction of the court, or the action must have occurred within the jurisdiction of the court

Claim limit: $5,000

Virginia

Name of court: District Court; listed under the name of the state or county, Claim division

Venue: Either the respondent must reside or do business within the jurisdiction of the court or the action must have occurred within the jurisdiction of the court

Claim limit: $5,000

Washington

Name of court: County District Court (and Justice Court in some areas); listed under name of county, District Court (or Justice Court)

Venue: The respondent must reside within the jurisdiction of the court

Claim limit: $500

West Virginia

Name of court: Magistrates Court, Small Claims; listed under name of county or under name of judge for Magistrates Court

Venue: The respondent must reside within the jurisdiction of the court

Claim limit: $1,500

Wisconsin

Name of court: Circuit Court; listed under County Government, Small Claims

Venue: The respondent must reside within
   the jurisdiction of the court
Claim limit: $1,000

Wyoming   Name of court: County Court and Justice of
                            the Peace Court; listed under name of
                            county, Small Claims, or specific justice
                            of the peace
                            Venue: Action must have occurred within
                               the jurisdiction of the court
                            Claim limit: $750

Appendix V

STATE POLICE PUBLIC INFORMATION CONTACTS

Consult your local directory for the currency and accuracy of addresses and telephone numbers.

ALABAMA DEPARTMENT
OF PUBLIC SAFETY
Alabama State Troopers
500 Dexter Avenue
Montgomery, Alabama
36130
(205) 832-5095

ALASKA DEPARTMENT OF
PUBLIC SAFETY
Alaska State Troopers
Information Officer
P.O. Box 6188 Annex
Anchorage, Alaska 99502
(907) 264-5560

ARIZONA DEPARTMENT OF
PUBLIC SAFETY
Arizona Highway Patrol
2310 North Twentieth Avenue
Phoenix, Arizona 85005
(602) 262-8011

ARKANSAS STATE POLICE
P.O. Box 4005
Little Rock, Arkansas 72203
(501) 371-2151

CALIFORNIA HIGHWAY
PATROL
Office of Public Affairs
P.O. Box 398
Sacramento, California 95804
(916) 445-3908

COLORADO STATE PATROL
Public Information Office
4201 East Arkansas Avenue
Denver, Colorado 80222
(303) 757-9636

CONNECTICUT STATE
POLICE
100 Washington Street
Hartford, Connecticut 06106
(203) 566-4054

DELAWARE STATE POLICE
Public Information Office
P.O. Box 430
Dover, Delaware 19901
(302)734-5973

DISTRICT OF COLUMBIA
Metropolitan Police Department
Public Information Office
300 Indiana Avenue NW
Washington, D.C. 20001
(202)626-2871

FLORIDA HIGHWAY
   PATROL
Public Information Section
Niel Kirkman Building
Tallahassee, Florida 32301
(904)488-7134

GEORGIA STATE PATROL
Public Information Office
959 East Confederate Avenue
Atlanta, Georgia, 30301
(404)656-6140

HONOLULU POLICE
   DEPARTMENT
1455 South Beretania Street
Honolulu, Hawaii 96814
(808)955-8111
Note: Hawaii has no Highway
   Patrol or State Police. County
   law enforcement agencies
   handle all traffic enforcement
   within their jurisdictions. This
   agency handles Honolulu City
   and County, which is the
   island of Oahu.

IDAHO STATE POLICE
P.O. Box 34
Boise, Idaho 83731
(208)384-3851

ILLINOIS STATE POLICE
Public Affairs Section
613 Armory Building
Springfield, Illinois 62706
(212)782-6637

INDIANA STATE POLICE
Public Information Office
100 North Senate Avenue
Indianapolis, Indiana 46204
(317)633-5674

IOWA HIGHWAY PATROL
Public Information Office
Wallace State Office Building
Des Moines, Iowa 50319
(515)281-8842

KANSAS HIGHWAY PATROL
Research and Planning Section
220 Gage Boulevard
Topeka, Kansas 66606
(913)296-3102

KENTUCKY STATE POLICE
Legal Section
Room 305
New State Office Building
Frankfort, Kentucky 40601
(502)564-4435

LOUISIANA STATE POLICE
Public Information Office
265 South Foster Drive
Baton Rouge, Louisiana 70802
(504)389-7300

MAINE STATE POLICE
Public Information Office
36 Hospital Street
Augusta, Maine 04333
(207)289-3033 or 289-3393

MARYLAND STATE POLICE
Public Information Office
Pikesville, Maryland 21208
(301)486-3101 Ext. 237

MASSACHUSETTS STATE
POLICE
State Police Headquarters
Traffic Division
Public Information Officer
1010 Commonwealth Avenue
Boston, Massachusetts 02215
(617)566-4500

MICHIGAN DEPARTMENT
OF STATE POLICE
Public Affairs Section
714 South Harrison Road
East Lansing, Michigan
48823
(517)373-8349

MINNESOTA STATE
POLICE
Information Desk
3800 Dunlap Street
St. Paul, Minnesota 55112
(612)482-5901

MISSISSIPPI HIGHWAY
SAFETY PATROL
Public Relations Bureau
P.O. Box 958
Jackson, Mississippi 39205
(601)982-1212 Ext. 220

MISSOURI STATE
HIGHWAY PATROL
Public Information Section
1510 East Elm Street
Jefferson City, Missouri 65101
(314)751-3313 Ext. 115

MONTANA DEPARTMENT
OF JUSTICE
Montana Highway Patrol
Bureau
1014 National Avenue
Helena, Montana 56901
(406)449-3000

NEBRASKA STATE PATROL
Public Information Office
P.O. Box 94907 State House
Lincoln, Nebraska 68509
(402)477-3951

NEVADA DEPARTMENT OF
MOTOR VEHICLES
Nevada Highway Patrol
555 Wright Way
Carson City, Nevada 89711
(702)885-5300

NEW HAMPSHIRE STATE
POLICE
Traffic Division
James Hayes Safety Building
Haven Drive
Concord, New Hampshire 03301
(603)271-3636

NEW JERSEY STATE POLICE
State Police Headquarters
Public Information Office
P.O. Box 7068
West Trenton, New Jersey 08625
(609)822-2000 Ext. 209

NEW MEXICO STATE
POLICE
Public Information Officer
Training Section
P.O. Box 1628
Santa Fe, New Mexico 87501
(505)827-5104

NEW YORK STATE
POLICE
Public Relations Supervisor
Building 22
State Campus
Albany, New York 12226
(518)456-6811

NORTH CAROLINA
HIGHWAY PATROL
Public Information Office
P.O. Box 27687
Raleigh, North Carolina 27611
(919)733-5027

NORTH DAKOTA HIGHWAY
PATROL
Public Information Section
State Capitol Building
Bismarck, North Dakota 58505
(701)224-2455

OHIO STATE HIGHWAY
PATROL
Planning and Research Section
660 East Main Street
Columbus, Ohio 43205
(614)466-3120

OKLAHOMA DEPARTMENT
OF PUBLIC SAFETY
Public Information Office
3600 North Eastern
Oklahoma City, Oklahoma
73136
(405)424-4011 Ext. 291

OREGON STATE POLICE
Public Information Office
107 Public Service Building
Salem, Oregon 97310
(503)378-3723

PENNSYLVANIA STATE
POLICE
Public Information Office
1800 Elmerton Avenue
Harrisburg, Pennsylvania
(717)783-5556

RHODE ISLAND
STATE POLICE
HEADQUARTERS
Public Information Office
P.O. Box 185
North Scituate, Rhode Island
02857
(401)647-3311

SOUTH CAROLINA
HIGHWAY PATROL
Public Information Section
955 Park Street
Columbia, South Carolina
29202
(803)758-2315

SOUTH DAKOTA HIGHWAY
PATROL
Deputy Director of Field
Operations
118 West Capitol Avenue
Pierre, South Dakota 57501
(605)773-3105

TENNESSEE DEPARTMENT
OF SAFETY
Public Relations and Information
Office
Room 1225
Andrew Jackson State Office
Building
Nashville, Tennessee 37219
(615)741-2491

TEXAS DEPARTMENT OF
PUBLIC SAFETY
Public Information Office
P.O. Box 4087
Austin, Texas 78773
(512)452-0331

UTAH HIGHWAY PATROL
Public Information Office
Room 304
State Office Building
Salt Lake City, Utah 84114
(801)533-5621

VERMONT DEPARTMENT
OF PUBLIC SAFETY
Vermont State Police
Public Information Office
Montpelier, Vermont 05602
(802)828-2187

VIRGINIA STATE POLICE
Public Information Office
P.O. Box 27472
Richmond, Virginia 23261
(804)272-1321 Ext. 269

WASHINGTON STATE
PATROL
Public Information Office
General Administration Building
Olympia, Washington 98504
(206)753-6562

WEST VIRGINIA STATE
POLICE
Public Information Officer
711 Jefferson Road
South Charleston, West Virginia
25309
(304)348-6370

WISCONSIN DEPARTMENT
OF TRANSPORTATION
Wisconsin State Patrol
Public Information Office
4802 Sheboygan Avenue
Madison, Wisconsin 53702
(608)266-7744

WYOMING HIGHWAY
PATROL
c/o Wyoming Highway
Department
Public Information Office
P.O. Box 1708
Cheyenne, Wyoming 82001
(307)777-7267

Bibliography

In General

Reference

Before You See a Lawyer, Robert Weber (New Century, 1981)
Looking at the Law, Neil Chayet (Rutledge Press, 1981)
What Every Woman Needs to Know about the Law, Martha Pomroy (Playboy Paperbacks, 1980)
Without a Lawyer, Steven Sarshik and Walter Szykita (New American Library, 1980)
The Complete Layman's Guide to the Law, John Paul Hanna (Prentice-Hall, 1974)
Lawyer's Desk Book (Institute for Business Planning, 1981)

There are various legal encyclopedias which attempt to cover all areas of the law in a relatively easy-to-read, straightforward manner. The two largest are *American Jurisprudence* (published and updated annually by the Lawyers' Cooperative Publishing Company) and *Corpus Juris Secundum* (published and updated annually by the West Publishing Company). West also puts out state law encyclopedias, as well as numerous handbooks in its "Nutshell" series (referred to below). The two most popular law dictionaries are *Black's* and *Ballentine's*; *Words and Phrases* is a multivolume service which provides definitions by courts of law.

Self-Help

Winning Your Personal Injury Suit, John Gunther (Anchor/Doubleday, 1980)

Winning with Your Attorney, Burton Marks and Gerald Goldfarb (McGraw-Hill, 1980)

The People's Law Review, edited by Ralph Warner (Addison-Wesley, 1980)

Getting What You Deserve, Nancy Kramer and Stephen Newman (Doubleday, 1979)

How to Handle Your Own Lawsuit, Jerome S. Rice (Contemporary Books, 1979)

How to Be Your Own Lawyer (Sometimes), Howard Eisenberg and Walter Kantrowitz (Perigee Books, 1979)

How to Deal Like a Lawyer in Person to Person Confrontations and Get Your Rights, Andrew Shapiro and John Striker (Rawson-Wade, 1979)

The New Consumer Survival Kit, Richard George (Little, Brown, 1978)

Your Property

Buying and Selling a House

Selling Your Home: A Guide to Getting the Best Price with or without a Broker, Carolyn Janik (Macmillan, 1980)

How to Sell Your House without a Broker, Harley Bjelland (Cornerstone Library, 1979)

Rights and Obligations of Debtors and Creditors

Bankruptcy Do It Yourself, Janice Kosel (Addison-Wesley, 1981)

Sum & Substance of Bankruptcy and Creditor's Rights, Douglas Boshkoff (Center for Creative Educational Services, 1980)

How to Get Your Creditors off Your Back without Losing Your Shirt, Melvin Kaplan (Contemporary Books, 1979)

Consumer Law: Cases and Materials, Ralph Rohner and John Spanogle (West, 1979)

Landlord-Tenant Relations

Landlord-Tenant Law in a Nutshell, David Hill (West, 1979)

Super Tenant: New York City Tenant Handbook, John Striker and Andrew Shapiro (Holt, Rinehart & Winston, 1978)

Your Family

Marriage and Divorce

Family Law in a Nutshell, Harry Krause (West, 1977)

Adoption and Guardianship

Law of Adoption, Morton Leavy (Oceana Legal Almanac Series, 1968)
The Rights of Parents, Martin Guggenheim and Alan Sussman (Avon, 1980)

Health Matters

The following are published by the Public Citizen Health Research Group and may be ordered from the Health Research Group, Department 109, 2000 P Street NW, Washington, D.C. 20036.

Winning at the Occupational Safety and Health Review Commission: A Worker's Handbook on Enforcing Safety and Health Standards, Marcia Goldberg (1981)
Medical Records: Getting Yours, Melissa Auerbach, Ted Bogue, and Maria Savath (1980)

Also:

The Rights of Hospital Patients (The Basic ACLU Guide to Hospital Patients' Rights), George Annas (Avon, 1975)
Human Rights and Health Care Law, Eugene Pavalon (1980)

Wills and Probate

Building Wealth: A Layman's Guide to Trust Planning, Adam Starchild (AMACOM, 1981)
You and Your Will, Paul Ashley (New American Library, 1977)
How to Avoid Probate, Norman F. Dacey (Crown, 1980)
How to Make a Will, How to Use Trusts, Parnell Callahan (Oceana, 1975)

Your Work

Employees' Rights

Federal Law of Employment Discrimination in a Nutshell, Mack Player (West, 1980)
Sue Your Boss, E. Richard Larson (Farrar, Straus, Giroux, 1981)

Starting a Business

Inc. Yourself: How to Profit by Setting Up Your Own Corporation, Judith H. McQuown (Warner Books, 1981)
Corporations in a Nutshell, Robert Hamilton (West, 1980)

Your Day in Court

Small Claims

You Can Win Big in Small Claims Court, James Morris (Rawson-Wade, 1981)
How You Can Sue without Hiring a Lawyer, Andrew Shapiro and John Striker (Simon & Schuster, 1981)
Everybody's Guide to Small Claims Court, Ralph Warner (Addison-Wesley, 1980)
Sue the Bastards, Douglas Matthews (Arbor House, 1973)

Traffic Violations

The Ticket Book, Rod Dornsife and Mark Miller (Ticket Books, Inc., 1978)

Using the Federal Government

Getting the Most Out of Washington, William Cohen and Kenneth Lasson (Facts on File, 1982)
Working on the System: A Comprehensive Manual for Citizen Access to Federal Agencies, Ralph Nader (Basic Books, 1974)

Various books are available on litigation under the federal Freedom of Information and Privacy Acts. Perhaps the most comprehensive reference tool is "Litigation under the Federal Freedom of Information Act and Privacy Act." The price for attorneys, government agencies, libraries, and institutions is $30; the price for tax-exempt organizations, students, and individual faculty members is $10. It may be ordered from the Center for National Security Studies, 122 Maryland Avenue NE, Washington, D.C. 20002.

Also available, and of greater use to laymen, is the eight-page pamphlet "The Freedom of Information Act: What It Is and How to Use It," which may be ordered free of charge from the Freedom of Information Clearinghouse, P.O. Box 19367, Washington, D.C. 20036.

Hiring a Lawyer

How to Hire a Lawyer: The Consumer's Guide to Good Counsel, Barry Gallagher (Delta/Seymour Lawrence, 1979)

KENNETH LASSON is a professor of law at the University of Baltimore and writes on a variety of subjects.

PUBLIC CITIZEN is a nonprofit citizen research, lobbying, and litigation organization based in Washington, D.C. Since its founding by Ralph Nader in 1971, Public Citizen has fought for consumer rights in the marketplace, for safe products, for a healthy environment and workplace, for clean and safe energy sources, and for corporate and government accountability.

Public Citizen is active in every public policy forum: Congress, the courts, government agencies, and the news media. They do not accept government or corporate grants. Their support funding comes from the sale of publications and from small individual contributions from citizens throughout the country who believe there should be full-time advocates of democratic principles working on their behalf. This support makes it possible for Public Citizen to challenge special-interest lobbying and the power of political action committees. Through their five affiliated groups, Public Citizen fights for citizens in numerous areas. *Congress Watch* monitors legislation on Capitol Hill and lobbies for the public interest. *The Health Research Group* fights for protections against unsafe foods, drugs, and workplaces, and for greater consumer control over health decisions. *The Litigation Group* brings precedent-setting lawsuits on behalf of citizens against the government and large corporations to enforce their rights and assure justice under the law. *The Tax Reform Group* advocates progressive tax reform and monitors the Internal Revenue Service. *The Critical Mass Energy Project* works for safe, efficient, and affordable energy.

Public Citizen
P.O. Box 19404
Washington, D.C. 20036